WAR
AGAINST THE
SAINTS

WAR
AGAINST THE
SAINTS

A BIBLICAL INSIGHT INTO OUR SPIRITUAL BATTLE

BILL RANDLES

LIGHTHOUSE TRAILS PUBLISHING
ROSEBURG, OREGON

WAR AGAINST THE SAINTS
© 2019 Bill Randles
First Lighthouse Trails Edition
Published by
Lighthouse Trails Publishing, Inc.
P.O. Box 307
Roseburg, Oregon 97470
www.lighthousetrails.com
All rights reserved. No part of this book may be reproduced, stored in a retrieval system, or transmitted in any form by any means, whether electronic, mechanical, photocopying, recordings, or otherwise without prior written permission from the publisher. Quotes and excerpts are permitted when in accordance with the U.S. Fair Use Act. Scripture quotations are taken from the *King James Version*. Cover and interior design by Lighthouse Trails. Cover photo and photo on page 78 from Alamy.com; used with permission. Illustration on page 111 from *Foxe's Book of Martyrs*; in public domain. Cover background from bigstockphoto.com; used with permission.

Publishers Cataloging-in-Publication Data

Randles, Bill
War Against the Saints
Includes bibliographical references and index.
1. Randles, Bill A. 2. Spiritual Battle 3. Christian--Doctrine. 4. Apologetics 5. Eschatology. I. Title.
   ISBN-13: 978-1-942423-43-0

PRINTED IN THE UNITED STATES OF AMERICA

Contents

Introduction 7

1/The Subtlety of the Serpent 11

2/The Ultimate Lie 17

3/The Very Heart of the Lie 23

4/What Is Antichrist? 31

5/Antichrist Will Spiritualize Jesus Christ 37

6/The New Gnostics 45

7/In the Power of the Wicked One 53

8/Temptation: The Underlying Religious Principle ... 59

9/Who Do the Kings of the Earth Serve? 73

10/The Serpent and the Dragon 81

11/The Warfare is Confessional 89

12/How People Deny Christ (Without Realizing It) ... 97

13/How We Win by Losing 103

    Armor of God 113

    Endnotes 115

    Scripture Index 119

    Other Resources 121

Introduction

And they worshipped the dragon which gave power unto the beast: and they worshipped the beast, saying, Who is like unto the beast? who is able to make war with him? And there was given unto him a mouth speaking great things and blasphemies; and power was given unto him to continue forty and two months. And he opened his mouth in blasphemy against God, to blaspheme his name, and his tabernacle, and them that dwell in heaven. *And it was given unto him to make war with the saints,* and to overcome them: and power was given him over all kindreds, and tongues, and nations. And all that dwell upon the earth shall worship him, whose names are not written in the book of life of the Lamb slain from the foundation of the world. (Revelation 13:4-8; emphasis added)

And of the ten horns that were in his head, and of the other which came up, and before whom three fell; even of that horn that had eyes, and a mouth that spake very great things, whose look

> was more stout than his fellows. I beheld, *and the same horn made war with the saints,* and prevailed against them; Until the Ancient of days came, and judgment was given to the saints of the most High; and the time came that the saints possessed the kingdom. (Daniel 7:20-22)

WHETHER WE BELIEVE IT and acknowledge it or not, the earth and the earth's inhabitants are all undergoing a tremendously intense level of spiritual warfare such as never seen before in history.

The Bible tells us that this acute, high-level spiritual warfare would be one of the characteristics of the last days. The Book of Revelation warns us that in the very end times, the Abyss (i.e., "the bottomless pit") will be opened, and the earth will be inundated by a locust-like demon invasion sent to torment all men. Paul warns us that in those last days, demons will invade even the church, teaching people doctrines which will cause many to fall away from the true faith.

God is allowing evil to come out into the open and to have a last hurrah, a final opportunity to fully manifest itself in the sight of all men, offering to fallen, deceived, Christ-rejecting mankind the kind of "world order" that Satan and his evil spirits have long promised as an option to the promise of the Kingdom of God.

This is truly their hour, the full expression of the power of darkness.

Thus shall Satan be given temporary permission to "make war" against the saints, (the holy people) and to overcome them. The fallen "god of this age" will be afforded

Introduction

a seeming string of "victories." For we are told the dragon wears many crowns (Revelation 12:3), and we shall realize soon that all worldly power and influence will be revealed to be at the service of the beast and utterly at his disposal.

During this time, the saints will have no worldly influence. They will be powerless to defend themselves when attacked in this world, and they will be impotent to set the record straight when they are lied about by the synagogue of Satan.

It is time for those of us who love and profess Jesus in this world to realize the spiritual warfare which wages about us so that we might engage properly. We need to see spiritually and to think from a spiritual perspective. Our war isn't against flesh and blood. People are not our true enemies. We can pray for those who have set themselves against us and overcome any evil they do against us, with good. We must hold to the truth and patiently await the ultimate triumph of the Seed of the woman. In many cases we will win by losing, for we "love not our lives unto death."

The adversary, Satan, is now operating against the church, using people, social systems, institutions, and technology to convey—right into our very minds—his philosophy, empty imaginations, and vain reasonings—knowledge that exalts itself against the knowledge of God. With modern technology, there has never been a better time for Satan to do this. For what better way to convey "images" than through our tablets and smart phones?

In this day and age, it is not uncommon that a child of (let's say) ten years old is given a little handheld portal to all of the knowledge, entertainment, and teaching in the world. Frequently, these things are handed over with little or no supervision. The technology represented by that Smart Phone exceeds the technology it took to land men on the moon.

How are we going to supervise this portal into our child's mind? Who is going to be there to counter the satanic propaganda, the lies, the false and distorted imagery, the anti-Christian narrative and interpretation of current events and history, the lionization of vile people, while at the same time demonizing people of faith?

This war against the saints will be non-stop until the Messiah comes to crush the serpent's head. The devil knows his time is short and that now is the time to seduce, cajole, and deceive as many people as possible away from God.

> Therefore rejoice, ye heavens, and ye that dwell in them. Woe to the inhabiters of the earth and of the sea! for the devil is come down unto you, having great wrath, because he knoweth that he hath but a short time. (Revelation 12:12)

CHAPTER ONE

THE SUBTLETY OF THE SERPENT

> Now the serpent was more subtle than any beast of the field which the LORD God had made. And he said unto the woman, Yea, hath God said, Ye shall not eat of every tree of the garden? (Genesis 3:1)

MANKIND HAS AN ADVERSARY, a malevolent being whose goal it is to estrange man from God and disrupt the peace and communion between God and man.

In the garden of Eden, in the first book of the Bible, he is simply introduced as "the serpent," and we are immediately impressed by the power of his subtlety. Thus, we can infer that this being was no mere snake. There is an intelligence and volition about him that mere reptiles are incapable of possessing though this malevolent being employed the serpent in his plan.

There is in Genesis no fuller introduction nor explanation as to his true identity. We would have to persevere all the way to the end of the Bible to find out the "serpent of old" was, in fact, the devil, and the ancient Satan (adversary)—a fallen angel cast out of Heaven.

> And the great dragon was cast out, that old serpent, called the Devil, and Satan, which deceiveth the whole world: he was cast out into the earth, and his angels were cast out with him. (Revelation 12:9)

He asked of the woman (not the man, whom God had appointed as head), a trick question.

What was he looking for when he inquired of the first couple?

He was looking for the smallest crack or opening between the couple and their God. Was there even a slight thread of alienation in the hearts of the first man and woman?

Thus, in his opening suggestion, the serpent greatly exaggerated the prohibition of God, *did God <u>really</u> ban you from eating of every tree in the garden?* The serpent knew this was an exaggeration, and he also knew the woman would know this was a gross exaggeration as well, for the question was but a probe into the mindset of the couple.

The woman's answer at first seemed to be adequate:

> And the woman said unto the serpent, We may eat of the fruit of the trees of the garden. (Genesis 3:2)

The Subtlety of the Serpent

She corrected the overstatement of the serpent, *God is not that strict! He has given us freedom to eat of the trees of the garden, but . . ."* She could have ended the conversation right there, but in that ". . . *but . . ."* she went on to reveal the slightest crack, a tiny seam of alienation of the couple from their benevolent Creator. Of course, it was nowhere near as overstated as in the serpent's initial question. They didn't think God was a tyrant . . . but . . .

> But of the fruit of the tree which is in the midst of the garden, God hath said, Ye shall not eat of it, neither shall ye touch it, lest ye die. (Genesis 3:3)

But what? Eve answered that God had forbidden them to eat of one tree (This was true), and furthermore He forbade them to even touch it . . . (This was false, a slight exaggeration of the strictness of God).

Next, she added a phrase which must have encouraged the serpent—"Lest ye die."

Lest ye die?

In other words, the woman was not so sure about the divine sanction. *Did God really say we would die? Or is it possible that we just might die, or that we might not die?*

God had originally told Adam, (who was to pass it on to Eve) that in the day they ate of the tree in the garden they would "surely die." It couldn't have been said any plainer or stronger than that, for God wanted them to know what was at stake.

Here was the opening the serpent had been waiting for. The conversation with the woman revealed the estrangement (ever so slight) of the couple, maximizing the prohibition of God, yet minimizing the penalty of God and outright calling it into question.

Now the serpent knew the first couple was ready to hear the Word of God openly denied. "Ye shall not surely die."

We see that this story is timeless and very modern, applicable to our own current situation. The serpent has long infiltrated the Christian churches and has been calling into question truths and doctrines which are obvious to any honest reader of Scripture. This is one of the ways he makes war against the saints.

The Christian teachings on marriage, gender, prohibitions against fornication, adultery, and all forms of perversion, as well as the Christian promise of Heaven to gain and Hell to be shunned, are clearly described in the Scriptures. There can be no mistaking the plain meaning of the texts.

What's more, almost all of the horrible things I know about Hell come from the lips of Jesus Himself. The doctrine of eternal conscious punishment is so horrible, it is as though God entrusted the bulk of descriptions of hellfire to His Son alone, so that no one could say, "Paul or Peter had a lot of hang-ups. That's why they railed about Hell!"

But Jesus is the one who taught us about "weeping and gnashing of teeth," "outer darkness," and an urgency to escape to the point where one would cut off his or her hand or foot to escape it!

THE SUBTLETY OF THE SERPENT

> The Son of man shall send forth his angels, and they shall gather out of his kingdom all things that offend, and them which do iniquity; And shall cast them into a furnace of fire: there shall be wailing and gnashing of teeth. . . . So shall it be at the end of the world: the angels shall come forth, and sever the wicked from among the just, And shall cast them into the furnace of fire: there shall be wailing and gnashing of teeth. (Matthew 13:41-42, 49-50)

> And if thy hand offend thee, cut it off: it is better for thee to enter into life maimed, than having two hands to go into hell, into the fire that never shall be quenched . . . Where their worm dieth not, and the fire is not quenched. For every one shall be salted with fire, and every sacrifice shall be salted with salt. (Mark 9:43, 48-49)

> Then said the king to the servants, Bind him hand and foot, and take him away, and cast him into outer darkness, there shall be weeping and gnashing of teeth. (Matthew 22:13)

> But the children of the kingdom shall be cast out into outer darkness: there shall be weeping and gnashing of teeth. (Matthew 8:12)

See how clear this teaching is? These are the words of Jesus! You wouldn't think it possible to deny such things in church, but there are many, many pastors and teachers who do so. They have listened to the serpent and put themselves unwittingly at his disposal to help carry out his program of distorting and denying the Word of God.

My point is that we are truly engaged in a real spiritual warfare.

We have a very subtle adversary; thus, we cannot afford to loosen our grip on the Word of God and walk by the inclination of our own fallen hearts. This is the master deceiver, the one who "deceiveth the whole world." He has tormented and taken advantage of many earnest and sincere Christians. We must put all of our trust in the Lord and His Word.

> Beloved, believe not every spirit, but try the spirits whether they are of God: because many false prophets are gone out into the world. Hereby know ye the Spirit of God: Every spirit that confesseth that Jesus Christ is come in the flesh is of God: And every spirit that confesseth not that Jesus Christ is come in the flesh is not of God: and this is that spirit of antichrist, whereof ye have heard that it should come; and even now already is it in the world. Ye are of God, little children, and have overcome them: because greater is he that is in you, than he that is in the world. (1 John 4:1-4)

CHAPTER TWO

THE ULTIMATE LIE

And then shall that Wicked be revealed, whom the Lord shall consume with the spirit of his mouth, and shall destroy with the brightness of his coming: Even him, whose coming is after the working of Satan with all power and signs and lying wonders, And with all deceivableness of unrighteousness in them that perish; because they received not the love of the truth, that they might be saved. And for this cause God shall send them strong delusion, that they should believe a lie: That they all might be damned who believed not the truth, but had pleasure in unrighteousness. (2 Thessalonians 2:8-12)

THE ADVERSARY OF MANKIND is a liar. He bore false witness against God to trick our parents into defecting from God, bringing ruin upon the human race. He wove a skillful lie when he seduced them into eating the forbidden fruit. And by lies, he has kept the children of Adam and Eve in bondage to this very day, alienating the human race from the Creator and Redeemer God. By his lies, he has "weakened [and destroyed] the nations."

> And the great dragon was cast out, that old serpent, called the Devil, and Satan, which deceiveth the whole world: he was cast out into the earth, and his angels were cast out with him. (Revelation 12:9)

> How art thou fallen from heaven, O Lucifer, son of the morning! how art thou cut down to the ground, which didst weaken the nations! (Isaiah 14:12)

In the passage in 2 Thessalonians I cited on the previous page, the text literally reads, ". . . that they should believe the Lie."—not "a lie."[1]

Though there are millions of "lies" of various shapes, sizes, and for untold billions of situations, the Bible warns us that all of mankind is susceptible to an ultimate Lie—the primal lie by which all men fell.

Man wants to believe the Lie because it flatters him. Society is gravitating to the full acceptance of this Lie. It finds its way into everything everywhere in human society; advertising, entertainment, philosophy, education, health care, religion (including apostate Christianity), technology, and the sciences all seem to confirm it in some way.

The Ultimate Lie

What is this *Lie* which has exerted such a strong pull on humanity ever since the Garden? Or we should ask, what are the components of the original Lie, for it is complex?

The Lie of the serpent has these specific components:

- **"Yea, hath God said . . .":** The Lie always begins by calling God's clear Word into question. What did God *really* say? Notice he doesn't openly deny the Word of God at first, nor does he confirm it. The serpent raises the question, opening the couple to second guessing God's Word. Over the last several decades, this lie has been promoted by our so-called Bible schools and by theologians who have literally deconstructed the Bible through "higher criticism" thus destroying the faith of untold thousands who have come under their pernicious influence.

- **"Ye shall not eat of every tree of the garden? . . .":** In other words, this God seems stricter and more exacting than is reasonable. The serpent questions the near total freedom that Adam and Eve were granted. He implies they are bound in some restrictive submission to God. The false equation is: The God of the Bible equals bondage. Man must break free from such restrictions, such as Judeo-Christian morality. The second Psalm teaches us that the "kings of the earth and their rulers" have embarked on a liberation crusade seeking to cast aside the "bonds" and "cords" of the Lord and His Christ. We are currently living in the wreckage of such "freedom" in our decadent and cruel society.

- **"Ye shall not surely die . . ."**: At some point, the Lie openly denies and contradicts the Word of God. God said in Genesis 2, "the day that thou eatest thereof thou shalt surely die."

This is the denial of the reality of death (in all of its forms) as the penalty for sin, and it is also a denial of the "second death," the final and irrevocable eternal judgment and punishment of the unrepentant wicked.

"Ye shall not surely die." This lie is communicated through the centuries throughout the entire world via the teachings of reincarnation, Spiritism, Universalism, belief in ghosts, and many other occult notions.

The cults all attack with vigor the teachings of Christ on the danger of hellfire, the final judgment, and the separation of the wicked and the righteous at the end. Satan would teach modern men that death is a natural process; it is our friend; it is a portal to other lives; and all go to the same place—anything but the moral teaching of Scripture that because God has ordained a moral universe, "[I]t is appointed unto men once to die, but after this the judgment" (Hebrews 9:27).

- **"For God doth know . . . your eyes shall be opened . . . ":** This is the master slander of the good and upright God. *The Creator knows something which He is keeping from you. It is something very fulfilling and beneficial, which He keeps to Himself, not wanting to share it with you and me.*

In this part of the Lie, the serpent is the illuminator, the guide into the hidden knowledge. He is the one who enlightens man and sets him free from the illusion into which the Creator has had man locked. No one wants to be in the dark. We all have a deep desire to be let in on the secret. This is why books such as *The Lost Books of the Bible* or *The Secrets of the Kingdom* will always appeal to a vast group of people. The very word *occult* means "hidden." The occult is currently experiencing an unprecedented revival. What is this secret of secrets which God has supposedly withheld from us? That . . .

- **"Ye shall be as gods, knowing good and evil . . .":** This is the very essence of the Lie. It is the mystery of iniquity which corrupts the human race and the treason against God by which unconverted man will be condemned forever, in spite of the redeeming love of God.

It is to this topic, the deification of man, that we must devote our attention in the next chapter.

Ye are my witnesses, saith the Lord, and my servant whom I have chosen: that ye may know and believe me, and understand that I am he: before me there was no God formed, neither shall there be after me. (Isaiah 43:10)

CHAPTER THREE

THE VERY HEART OF THE LIE

> Now the Spirit speaketh expressly, that in the latter times some shall depart from the faith, giving heed to seducing spirits, and doctrines of devils; Speaking lies in hypocrisy; having their conscience seared with a hot iron; Forbidding to marry, and commanding to abstain from meats, which God hath created to be received with thanksgiving of them which believe and know the truth. (1 Timothy 4:1-3)

IN THE LATE 1950s, an atheistic medical psychologist named Helen Schucman began to receive strange dreams and odd promptings to write down dictation from a disembodied voice. Eventually, one of her colleagues urged her to go ahead and write it all down, and he would edit it. Out of this occult experience came the very popular book *A Course in Miracles*. It consists of three books: a

622-page text, a 478-page workbook for students, and an 88-page manual for teachers, all given by the occult practice of automatic writing or channeling. From the *Course's* Preface:

> Three startling months preceded the actual writing, during which time Bill suggested that I write down the highly symbolic dreams and descriptions of the strange images that were coming to me. Although I had grown more accustomed to the unexpected by that time, I was still very surprised when I wrote, "This is a course in miracles." That was my introduction to the Voice. It made no sound, but seemed to be giving me a kind of rapid, inner dictation which I took down in a shorthand notebook. The writing was never automatic. It could be interrupted at any time and later picked up again. It made me very uncomfortable, but it never seriously occurred to me to stop. It seemed to be a special assignment I had somehow, somewhere agreed to complete.[2]

This book has gone on to be translated in more than 23 languages and is globally distributed and promoted by people such as Oprah Winfrey and Democrat presidential candate for 2020, Marianne Williamson.

What is it that "the Voice," which dictated to the atheistic professor has to say? Here are a few direct quotes from the *Course in Miracles* voice:

> God is in everything I see. (Vol. 2, p. 45)

God is still everywhere and in everything forever. And we are a part of Him. (Vol. 1, p. 92)

Whenever you question your value, say: "God Himself is incomplete without me." (Vol. 1, p. 165)

The recognition of God is the recognition of yourself. There is no separation of God and His creation. (Vol. 1, p. 136)

This is the serpent's lie, repackaged, updated, and very popular in the age of Oprah and Doctor Phil. By loving and clinging to this lie, many will never know the true God or His free gift of salvation based on the Cross to those who acknowledge their need of a Savior because of their sinfulness.

I want to use this book (*A Course in Miracles*) as an example of a larger end-times movement of massive deception, which Satan has unleashed upon the Earth in these last days. He knows his time is short, and he will deceive as many sons and daughters of Adam as possible to damn them and send them to Hell.

To truly engage in spiritual warfare, we must take the time to understand the teaching and philosophies which hold men back from being saved. The apostle Paul calls it, "Casting down vain imaginations and every high thing which exalts itself against the knowledge of God." Today's world is being heavily drawn into pantheism (the belief that all is God), and most believers are unaware this is happening.

A Course in Miracles, and the movement of which it is representative, flies in the face of a very important distinction found in the first verse of the Bible ("In the beginning God created . . ."). The blurring of this distinction is at the heart of every false religion and is the very corruption of the human race. I speak of the Creator/creature distinction.

All is not one, as *A Course in Miracles*, Buddhists, New Agers, and Hindus claim. Satan's warfare against mankind lies in part in blurring that distinction.

All is two. "God created the heavens and the earth . . ." and that is all there really is—God and His creation.

The Christian church (and Judaism before it) bore witness to this distinction, insisting on the absolute transcendence of the Creator. He alone is God; there is no other. Creation came from Him but is in no way a part of Him. We ourselves are created, dependent beings.

There is God and His creation, two distinct categories. God is eternal and self-existent. Creation had a beginning and will have its end, and it depends upon God for its existence. God has no limits, but creation is limited by time, space, and matter.

In Genesis 3, Satan's lie blurred that distinction when he told Adam and Eve they too could be as gods . . . as though attaining godhood was merely a matter of partaking of whatever it was of which God partook. He denied the transcendence of God, putting everything on the same level, and implying that there is a secret to attaining godhood.

The name for this error is pantheism, the belief that God is inseparable from all of His creation, and that God is in everything, or that everything is God.

Pantheism is as ancient as the fall of man in Genesis 3, but it was dealt a setback when the Lord revealed Himself to Israel and then to the church. Belief in the transcendent Creator/Redeemer God became the foundation for Western Civilization with all of its blessing. We knew from the Bible the creation is not divine. It is no mystery. It can be studied and understood according to predictable laws because it is the creation of a personal God. However, lately the West has gone Eastern.

Pantheism is rapidly spreading across the world as the Judeo-Christian world lets go of its former faith to embrace Eastern religions such as Hinduism, Yoga, or the New Age. This error lies as a subtext beneath many popular movies such as *Star Wars* with its impersonal force, or *The Matrix* which teaches the created world is but an illusion.

What did the God of Creation set about doing after Creation? He set about dividing things, light from darkness, male from female, water from land, the waters above from the waters below, and day and night. But those who deny this have set about removing all distinctions. This explains the madness of our postmodern, decadent society. The radical egalitarianism we are seeing in the "gender wars" and the deliberate confusion of sexual roles is a reflection of this false belief, because pantheism is a war on all distinctions.

Schucman's demonically inspired book has been an effective weapon in Satan's arsenal, bringing pantheism to the forefront of contemporary thinking. I will select a few quotes from *A Course in Miracles*, for its teachings are very instructive to us, and we can see what many well-meaning people are believing and practicing as they are blinded into a false spirituality spawned by Satan and his servants.

> Equals should not be in awe of one another because awe implies inequality. It is therefore an inappropriate reaction to me. An elder brother is entitled to respect for his greater experience, and obedience for his greater wisdom . . . There is nothing about me that you cannot attain. (vol. 1, p. 5)

> My mind will always be like yours, because we were created as equals. It was only my decision that gave me all power in heaven and earth. My only gift to you is to help you make the same decision. (vol. 1, p. 70-71)

The *Course's* "Jesus" insists he is equal to the rest of us, that there is nothing different about him; he is only here to show us the right decisions. One of the implications of pantheism is the negation of the concept of sin. There can be no right or wrong if "all is one," and "good and evil" are only constructs. There is no Heaven or Hell or judgment in the systems of pantheism. Therefore, pantheism negates the need for salvation, redemption, or any kind of propitiation (sacrifice for sin). Sin is a mere illusion, correctible by positive thoughts.

> No one is punished for sins, and the Sons of God are not sinners. (vol. 1, p.88)

> The Holy Spirit will never teach you that you are sinful. (vol. 1, p. 423)

THE VERY HEART OF THE LIE

> When you are tempted to believe that sin is real, remember this: If sin is real, both God and you are not. (vol. 1, p. 377)

Therefore, the need and efficacy of the crucifixion of Jesus is also denied in this best-selling metaphysical book, promoted by influential people such as Oprah Winfrey and Eckhardt Tolle. Truly, Satan is making war on the Gospel, attacking the message itself and lying to the world about the only way to be saved.

> A slain Christ has no meaning. But a risen Christ becomes the symbol of the Son of God's forgiveness on himself; the sign he looks upon himself as healed and whole. (vol. 1, p. 396)

Obviously, there need be no Hell or final judgment if sin is but an illusion, and we are all a part of "god."

> The Holy Spirit teaches thus: There is no hell. Hell is only what the ego has made of the present. (vol. 1, p. 281)

These quotes have illustrated the nature of the Lie that many have been seduced into loving and believing. By it, they have rejected reality as well as the only true God and Father of our Lord Jesus Christ.

This is the Lie which Satan has sold to our generation. It is the new "gnosis," the secret knowledge, which (falsely) claims to be more genuine, more compassionate, more open-minded, loving, and tolerant than the gospel-believing church has ever been in history.

One day these peace-loving pagans will turn on those who hold to the truth, and we will see how cruel their "tender mercies" really are. Beware the intolerance of the tolerant!

CHAPTER FOUR

WHAT IS ANTICHRIST?

> Beloved, believe not every spirit, but try the spirits whether they are of God: because many false prophets are gone out into the world. Hereby know ye the Spirit of God: Every spirit that confesseth that Jesus Christ is come in the flesh is of God: And every spirit that confesseth not that Jesus Christ is come in the flesh is not of God: and this is that spirit of antichrist, whereof ye have heard that it should come; and even now already is it in the world. (1 John 4:1-3)

WHY DID I CALL this chapter "What is Antichrist?" rather than perhaps the more provocative, "Who is Antichrist?" I wanted to establish that it is the entire concept called "antichrist" that Satan uses to wage war on Israel (the Jews) and the saints. This concept manifests itself chiefly in three entities: the spirit of antichrist, the many antichrists already in the world, and ultimately this will culminate in an individual, the Antichrist, who comes at the end of the world.

The word *antichrist* is compound. The prefix, *anti* is added to the word *Christ*. The word *Christ* is a Greek term for the Hebrew word *Messiah*, i.e. "The Anointed One."

Jesus is the Christ of God, the one promised from the very beginning, the "Seed of the woman," the "Seed of Abraham," "the star that comes out of Jacob," the "root of Jesse," the "Son of David," the one promised by all of the prophets since the third chapter of Genesis. He, Jesus of Nazareth, alone, met all of the credentials outlined in the constant promise to Israel that God would send a Messiah.

He would be born in Bethlehem, Ephratah as Micah 5:2 predicted. He would come shortly before the Temple was destroyed (as promised in Daniel 9:25-27) and at the very time that *the scepter departed from Judah* as Jacob predicted in Genesis 49. David saw the crucifixion of the Anointed One but prophesied in Psalm 22 that He would live again. Isaiah prophesied He would be sacrificed "with the wicked" (as fulfilled in the two thieves) and buried in a rich man's tomb (Isaiah 53:9).

You would have to be very obtuse and resistant to God to keep on denying that Jesus is the Christ, the Messiah, in the face of such undeniable fulfilled prophecies.

But for all of those who insist upon rejecting Jesus, another messiah, "anointed one" will soon appear.

Jesus stated that those who refuse to accept Him (the One who actually met the criterion) will be presented with another who doesn't bother to meet the criterion nor even appear to do so. He comes "in his own name," and they will receive him instead.

> I am come in my Father's name, and ye receive me not: if another shall come in his own name, him ye will receive. (John 5:43)

This is the concept of antichrist. The prefix *anti* means "in the place of" or as "a substitute" for Christ. Antichrist doesn't mean "against Christ"; it means "instead of Christ."

Jesus Christ, the Messiah, sent His Spirit into the world upon His resurrection to empower the church and to form a bride for Himself (the Bride of Christ) and to witness to the world of sin, righteousness, and judgment.

The false spirit—the spirit of antichrist—has been released to do something similar, but opposite. He, the spirit of antichrist, is forming a body of false Christians, a bride of antichrist steeped in mysticism, experienced-based Christianity, false prophecy, and a distorted "grace doctrine" which actually gives license to sin and denies the reality of a final punishment.

I have seen this "anti-anointing" and written about it in several books.[3] An artificial Pentecost occurred in 1994 when the "spirit" overtook worshippers at the Toronto Airport Vineyard in Ontario, Canada putting them into trances and inducing them into a state called "spiritual drunkenness." This phenomenon became widely known, and thousands of Christians made pilgrimage to Toronto to "soak" in the "blessing" and then to carry it home to their churches.

This "new anointing" empowered pastors to quit preaching the Word, to seek to be intoxicated in the "new wine," and to write sensual songs to Jesus and the Father in the name of the "spirit."

One main proponent of the movement, Rodney Howard Browne, became known as "God's Bartender," and he called his meetings, "Joel's Place," as if the prophet Joel had opened a pub for drinking!

This so-called "revival" was accepted and promoted by hundreds of thousands of Christians throughout Europe, England, America, Canada, and other English-speaking regions. The Assemblies of God stood against it until they received their own version of it called the "Pensacola Revival," another supposed "revival" at an Assembly of God church in Brownsville, Florida.[4] This particular "revival" sparked a signs and wonders apostasy that has had negative repercussions throughout the world wherein the preaching of the Gospel has been largely supplanted by strange manifestations thought to be from God though lacking the genuine fruit of the Holy Spirit.[5]

The last days will be marked by the outpouring of a counterfeit holy spirit. A lawless Pentecost will occur, and men will be deceived by signs and wonders which come after the working of Satan. It will also be accompanied by a strong delusion sent by God:

> Even him, whose coming is after the working of Satan with all power and signs and lying wonders, And with all deceivableness of unrighteousness in them that perish; because

> they received not the love of the truth, that they might be saved. And for this cause God shall send them strong delusion, that they should believe a lie: That they all might be damned who believed not the truth, but had pleasure in unrighteousness. (2 Thessalonians 2:9-12)

A spirit of antichrist has been poured out upon the world to rival the Holy Spirit of Christ.

There are also many individual antichrists, which have come and which will come into the world. Antichrists are false christs who supplant a real walk with Jesus by false teachings designed to redefine the knowledge of God. False "Christian" teachers and so-called prophets are antichrists. They rob people of real faith by teaching pseudo-faith.

I had been converted for only a few months when I was exposed to the teaching of Kenneth Copeland and Kenneth Hagin, two very popular charismatic teachers in the 1970s. Both of these teachers purported to be "Word" or "Word of Faith" teachers. They seemed down-to-earth in their communication, thus very appealing and homespun with Texas accents and impressive oration skills.

However, their teachings amount to a redefinition of the Fall: Man lost dominion and authority, granting it to Satan. They redefine faith itself: Faith is a force, operating by set laws; God uses faith to create; God Himself is under the laws of faith.[6] They teach that Jesus' death on the Cross was inadequate to save us.[7] First, He had to descend into Hell to be tortured by Satan until He had paid the price for our sins; only then could He be raised from death.[8]

They also teach that we, the redeemed sons of God, are in fact "little gods," in "God's class of being" and "as much an incarnation as the incarnation of Jesus Christ."[9]

When God opened my eyes to the Word of Faith error, I had a choice to make; I had to either admit I had been wrong and back away from these heretics and their teachings or just stay in the movement. I had to ask myself, *am I a little god? Isn't that the serpent's lie in the garden?*

By repenting of the false teachings I had so happily received, I actually "overcame" the antichrists.

> Ye are of God, little children, and have overcome them: because greater is he that is in you, than he that is in the world. They are of the world: therefore speak they of the world, and the world heareth them. (1 John 4:4-5)

CHAPTER FIVE

ANTICHRIST WILL SPIRITUALIZE JESUS CHRIST

Beloved, believe not every spirit, but try the spirits whether they are of God: because many false prophets are gone out into the world. Hereby know ye the Spirit of God: Every spirit that confesseth that Jesus Christ is come in the flesh is of God: And every spirit that confesseth not that Jesus Christ is come in the flesh is not of God: and this is that spirit of antichrist, whereof ye have heard that it should come; and even now already is it in the world. Ye are of God, little children, and have overcome them: because greater is he that is in you, than he that is in the world. They are of the world: therefore speak they of the world, and the world heareth them. We are of God: he that knoweth God heareth us; he that is not of God heareth not us. Hereby know we the spirit of truth, and the spirit of error. (1 John 4:1-6)

War Against the Saints

THE SAINTS OF GOD are rejected in this world by an unholy trinity. The *Holy* Trinity is, of course, the Father, Son, and Holy Ghost. Raging against this true Holy Trinity and against the saints are the world, the flesh, and the devil—that serpent of old.

The flesh lusts against the spirit. The devil resisted the coming of the Son of God. And those who have succumbed to the love of this world have none of the love of the Father in their hearts.

We see here the antichrist spirit is also called "the spirit of error" (1 John 4:6) which is obviously opposed to the truth, revealed and propagated by the Holy Spirit.

What specifically does the Bible mean by the expression *the truth*? Is this a general or specific term when used in Scripture? Are we talking about *all* truth (e.g., mathematics, science, physics, history, current events)? Or simple veracity? When Jesus proclaimed before Pontius Pilate that His mission was to "bear witness unto the truth," He was not referring to truth in general.

> Pilate therefore said unto him, Art thou a king then? Jesus answered, Thou sayest that I am a king. To this end was I born, and for this cause came I into the world, that I should *bear witness unto the truth*. Every one that is of the truth heareth my voice. (John 18:37)

The Bible is true and never wrong in anything it says about history, the natural world, physics, etc. But *the Truth* is a more specific and even a Theo-technical term.

Antichrist will Spiritualize Jesus Christ

The Truth refers to the only sure depiction of spiritual reality—who we are as humans, why we are here, what went wrong with the world, what sin is, who God is, how we can be reconciled to Him, what happens after death. Most important of all, the Truth is the incarnation of God in the person of Christ who came to save us from our sins.

How would man know any of the answers to any of the above questions without a revelation from God Himself? We can learn a lot of things about this created world by observation and experiment (science), and it is the province of man to search them out since man is still the (fallen) regent of creation.

But only God can show me that I am a sinner, that there is a Heaven and a Hell, and that this is a moral universe—thus, there is a final judgment for all of us. We would have to take His word for it; there is no way we could discover these things on our own.

The core of the Truth is the incarnation, that God became a man in the person of Jesus Christ. Heaven and Earth cannot reveal this to us, but the Father in Heaven testifies to it. The incarnation of Jesus is the core of the divine revelation. It is the answer to the problem of sin and men's alienation from God—God became a man, a real man.

The man hanging between Heaven and Earth on the Cross of the curse, and wearing the crown of the very curse of God, was none less than the second Person of the Godhead.

How could God die? Only by becoming a man.

Why did He have to die? Because His own justice demands death for sin, "The wages of sin is death . . ." (Romans

6:23). But "Christ also hath once suffered for sins, the just for the unjust, that he might bring us to God" (1 Peter 3:18).

> Who his own self bare our sins in his own body on the tree, that we, being dead to sins, should live unto righteousness: by whose stripes ye were healed. (1 Peter 2:24)

Jesus Christ is God come to us in the flesh—hanging on a real cross of wood, wearing a crown of thorns, suffering immensely, and dying physically on a specific calendar day in history.

This is how the devil attacks the faith of the church. He denies the incarnation in some way; he seeks to make Jesus into an abstract concept, a symbol, perhaps an exceptional human being, or as some in the emerging church put it, a "servant leader" (i.e., someone who is a good example to follow) but not God in the flesh.

What John literally says in the passage from 1 John 4 is "Every spirit that confesses that Jesus Christ has come (and remains) in the flesh is of God." As I wrote in my book, *Mending The Nets*—

> The gospel accounts of the crucifixion and resurrection have a markedly physical emphasis. We are told that the cross is wooden, the dying Jesus is thirsty, when pronounced dead by the guards, His side is pierced with a spear, and blood and water flow out. The disciples have to pry Jesus' dead body off the cross, spices are used

> to embalm Jesus' body, and a stone is rolled over the mouth of the tomb.
>
> On that first Easter morning, the disciples race to the tomb and have to stoop to enter it. We are told that when they saw the embalming clothes, they believed. Jesus appeared to them and told them not to handle Him. When He ate fish with them, they would not have been able to see the fish through his esophagus, since He was in the flesh and not a spirit.[10]

Certain false teachers had arisen in the earliest stages of church history. They were called "Gnostics" or "knowing ones" because they believed they knew something spiritual the rest of the church didn't know. They had a secret revelation which elevated them beyond simple Christianity as taught by the apostles. These deceivers redefined Christianity to conform to Greek philosophy. In Plato's cosmology, the physical realm is evil, the creator of the physical world was an evil god, and salvation means release from all physical bounds.

Some Gnostics taught that Jesus didn't really incarnate, He only seemed to. (This is Docetism, meaning "seemed to"). There are Gnostic gospels, which feature a Jesus who makes no footprints in the sand and is ethereal and even see-through. He didn't really "suffer, die, and was buried" but only seemed to. The apostle John appears to be countering this heresy in his epistle.

We also encounter another form of this heresy called "Adoptionism." This doctrine taught that Jesus was an ordinary human being who was anointed at His baptism (Christed); and this "anointing" only remained with Him until the crucifixion, where it lifted, and He went back to being a mere human being. In other words, He was only "Christed" between the water and the blood. John refutes this when he says that through the Holy Spirit Jesus, the Christ of God, "came by water and by blood." He came into the world as the Christ of God and never ceased being the Christ of God through His death, burial, resurrection, and ascension to Heaven.

> Who is he that overcometh the world, but he that believeth that Jesus is the Son of God? This is he that came by water and blood, even Jesus Christ; not by water only, but by water and blood. And it is the Spirit that beareth witness, because the Spirit is truth. (1 John 5:5-6)

However, antichrist seeks to deny this central revelation from God. Why?

If antichrist can "spiritualize Jesus" then anything can represent "Jesus"—false prophets, false revivals, deluding spirits, deluded people who believe they too are as anointed as Jesus was.

The spiritualization of Christ and of Christianity is a prime component of the coming demonic deception soon to be perpetrated by the Antichrist and the coming army of deceivers, seducers, and apostates.

When people spiritualize Christ and let go of the reality that Jesus Christ is a real man who came in the flesh, they

Antichrist will Spiritualize Jesus Christ

then spiritualize the rest of the Bible also. They produce spiritualized love and spiritualized righteousness as well.

They do not end up truly loving individual people in deed and in truth; rather, they "love everyone in the world" with an "unconditional love" that is ethereal and abstract; perhaps it even gives them ecstatic feelings, but it isn't real in a concrete sense.

The same goes for their righteousness. They do not live under the impetus of the law of Christ, which calls for real righteousness (that can only come from Christ) and true repentance of individual sins and lawlessness. Rather, their righteousness is merely spiritual or ethereal in the sense that it has no tangible connection with how one lives. It is "who they are" and not in any way dependent on a relationship of obedience and trust.

In the Gnostic scheme, since the physical world isn't as significant as the spiritual world, it doesn't matter what one does physically. They believe that sins of the flesh do not alter a person's spirituality.

Because of this over spiritualization of Christianity, many are untroubled by obvious false prophets such as Todd Bentley, who left his wife and children for his secretary. In spite of this, he still goes about giving people "words" and "healing them," as he preaches ridiculous "sermons," which really are nothing but empty anecdotes of his experiences with angels, demons, and even "Jesus." But people show up in the thousands to be "blessed" and "anointed" by Bentley and to receive prophetic "words."

Their righteousness is only spiritual, as is their love, because their Jesus is also a mere spirituality, not a real, concrete person who came and remains in the flesh. He is an abstract figure in dreams and imaginations but makes no moral demands because in the Gnostic way of thinking, actual sin doesn't hurt your relationship with God; all that matters is "who you are" in Christ.

They would do well to heed John the apostle on this point for they have departed from the Truth.

> Little children, let no man deceive you: he that doeth righteousness is righteous, even as he is righteous. He that committeth sin is of the devil; for the devil sinneth from the beginning. For this purpose the Son of God was manifested, that he might destroy the works of the devil. (1 John 3:7-8)

CHAPTER SIX

THE NEW GNOSTICS

> I have not written unto you because ye know
> not the truth, but because ye know it, and that
> no lie is of the truth. (1 John 2:21)

THE CHURCH IS UNDERGOING perhaps her final assault from within, as she has been beset with a new wave of Gnostics who have entered in.

What is Gnosticism? One definition of Gnosticism states:

> Gnosticism was built on Greek philosophy that taught matter was evil and the Spirit was good. . . . So-called "Christian Gnostics" said since matter was evil, God could not really incarnate in a human body; He only appeared in human form and only appeared to suffer, but basically, it was an illusion. . . .

> Prior to Christianity, the Gnostics taught that man is composed of body, soul, and spirit. The body and the soul are man's earthly existence and were considered evil. Enclosed in man's soul is the spirit, a divine substance of man. This "spirit" was asleep and ignorant and needed to be awakened. It could only be liberated by a special knowledge that would be later called "illumination."[11]

The apostle Paul saw that Gnostic influences were coming into the church, and he addressed them in his epistles (Colossians 2:8-23, 1 Timothy 1:4, 2 Timothy 2:16-19, and Titus 1:10-16).

Gnostics ("knowing ones") redefined the knowledge of God (i.e., what it means to know and communicate with God). They were elitists who sought "deeper knowledge" than that which is revealed in God's Word. Gnostics despised doctrine, dismissing it as mere head knowledge.

They held forth a view of "salvation" which was, in fact, merely a self-realization rather than the rescue from sin and judgment through the blood of Jesus (which the Bible says is the only means of atoning for sin).

Gnostics believed that self-realization wasn't for every Christian but only available to elite Christians who are let in on the secret knowledge (the so-called "secrets of the kingdom" available only to the initiated). The same attacks are presently being launched as dogma also. The "dry, dusty doctrines of another day" are being jettisoned by the "new" Gnostics of today who eagerly covet "new revelation" or "present truth."

The New Gnostics

Gnostics influenced me early in my walk with Jesus. I was given a pack of Kenneth Copeland and Kenneth Hagin teachings and entered into the "deep revelations" of the Word Faith heresy. I learned such "revelations" as the following: the believer is just as much an incarnation as Jesus was, faith is a force, and we all can learn to use the *laws of faith* to get what we need. (If this were true, we wouldn't need God; we would simply learn the laws of faith and control it like the force.)

The deepest, darkest core of the Gnostic teaching was that we believers are in "God's class of being." In other words, "we are little gods" who just don't realize it yet.

According to the modern Gnostics, Jesus Himself was a man of faith upon whom the Holy Spirit came. He knew all of the laws of faith, which was why He could die on the Cross. Anyone could do so if he or she had the same "revelation knowledge" as Jesus.

Kenneth Copeland, the Word Faith preacher, is certainly one of today's Gnostics. Here is a sampling of some of his teachings:

> Every prophet that walked the face of the earth under the Abrahamic covenant could have paid the price if it were a physical death only. When He said "It is finished" on that cross, He was not speaking of the plan of redemption. The plan of redemption had just begun; there were still three days and three nights to be gone through.[12]

> The Spirit of God spoke to me and He said, "Son, realize this. Now follow me in this and

> don't let your tradition trip you up." He said, "Think this way—a twice-born man whipped Satan in his own domain." And I threw my Bible down . . . like that. I said, "What?" He said, "A born-again man defeated Satan, the firstborn of many brethren defeated him." He said, "You are the very image, the very copy of that one." I said, "Goodness, gracious sakes alive!" And I began to see what had gone on in there, and I said, "Well now you don't mean, you couldn't dare mean, that I could have done the same thing?" He said, "Oh yeah, if you'd had the knowledge of the Word of God that He did, you could have done the same thing, 'cause you're a reborn man too."[13]

What blasphemy! A whole generation of Christians have been swept away and corrupted on the deepest level by accepting this man's unbiblical teachings.

John Wimber was a Quaker who came into the charismatic movement. He eventually taught a famous course at Fuller Seminary, MC510 "Signs, Wonders, and Church Growth," which launched a "signs and wonders" movement that spread Gnostic teachings throughout the Earth. Eventually, this movement became the Vineyard Fellowship.

Of interest for this book is that Wimber taught that a "paradigm shift" in thinking was necessary to bring the church into "power evangelism." In my book, *Weighed and Found Wanting*, I explain:

> Wimber, Kraft, White and Williams, as well as many other Third Wave teachers, have been

The New Gnostics

calling for a "paradigm shift" for some time now . . . A paradigm shift is a total exchange of your world view! . . . What is the shift? It is from a primarily Western, rational, logical, objective point of view to an Eastern, subjective, experiential paradigm. Haven't we been subtly taught over the years that the Western mind set is cold, calculated, rational, based on just the observable facts? On the other hand, allegedly, the Eastern is mystical, from the heart, and based on experience?

Wimber teaches, "We must remember always that the Bible was written in the Middle East, not with rational assumption, that we bring to it as we try to understand it, but with an experiential assumption."[14] I interpret him to be saying that the Bible is not so much an objective book, but a subjective one. Not so much for understanding God mentally, but for experiencing Him intimately.

In another tape, Wimber explains: "You tell someone from the Far or Middle East that cotton only grows in warm semi-arid climates. England is cold and wet. [Ask them] Does cotton grow in England? The answer you'll get is, 'I don't know, I haven't been to England.'" Or, "I can't say unless I've been there, (experience)."[15] This is the new paradigm, a down playing of doctrine or "head knowledge" in favour of mystical experience. Another variation of this is, "God is bigger than His written word," translated, God wants to bring you into experiences that aren't in the limits of scripture. Just knowing God "doctrinally" is not sufficient, you now must have self-authenticating experiences. All of these attitudes are the end result of the New Paradigm. This is the shift from primarily objective to subjective thinking in our approach to truth.[16]

Perhaps the premier proponent of Gnosticism in the evangelical and charismatic church these days is Bill Johnson, the senior pastor of Bethel Church in Redding, California. Johnson's church is the current version of the Toronto Airport Vineyard and Brownsville Assembly of God *pilgrimage* sites where people influenced by Gnosticism come to "experience" God.

Through Bethel and most notably through their worship team (a popular rock band called "Jesus Culture"), Bethel reaches hundreds of thousands with its Gnostic message of anti-doctrinal, experience-based, New Age-emulating *power evangelism*.

I believe Bethel literally represents the final stages of the apostasy, the slide into the occult which I wrote about in the revised version of my book, *Beware the New Prophets*.

Here is an example of this redefinition of Christianity and the knowledge of God in occult terms promoted by Gnostics such as those associated with Bethel. An article in *The Christian Post* titled "Bethel Responds to Christian Tarot Cards Controversy" reported that Bethel "was accused of working with a Melbourne, Australia-based group known as Christalignment, which claims to have worked with many churches in that country to do such readings."*17* According to the article, Bethel denied using "Christian tarot cards." The article stated:

> Bethel admitted the leaders of Christalignment, Ken and Jenny Hodge, are connected with several of their church members as the Hodges are the parents to church evangelist Ben Fitzgerald, and said the church leaders "have a value for what they are seeking to accomplish."
>
> "They (Christalignment) stand in agreement with the Scriptures that all occult practices (like tarot cards) have no place in the Kingdom and should not be used," Bethel said in a statement.
>
> Christ Alignment staff describe themselves as "trained spiritual consultants," and say on their website that they "draw from the same divine energy of the Christ spirit."*18*

Christ Alignment staff further stated that,

> We practice a form of supernatural healing that flows from the universal presence of the Christ. We draw from the same divine energy of the Christ spirit, as ancient followers did and operate only out of the third heaven realm to gain insight and revelation.*19*

Satan has seduced large segments of the professing church into Gnosticism and the occult. Like King Saul in the last desperate hours of his life, some have gone into darkness seeking power and a "word" of comfort, having already rejected the true Word of God.

CHAPTER SEVEN

Lying in the Power of the Wicked One

> And we know that we are of God, and the whole world lieth in wickedness. And we know that the Son of God is come, and hath given us an understanding, that we may know him that is true, and we are in him that is true, even in his Son Jesus Christ. This is the true God, and eternal life. Little children, keep yourselves from idols. Amen. (1 John 5:19-21)

WE CANNOT DO A study of Satan's war against the saints without facing the reality of which the apostle John warns—that the whole world lies in the power of the wicked one. What does this expression mean?

The *world* here does not refer to the Earth; it refers to the way all of humanity has organized itself to the exclusion of God. Man is in flight from God and has always sought to make for himself an Eden without submission and devotion to God. Every society on this Earth reflects this reality in different ways, whether it be the Islamic Ulema, the Hindu and Buddhist world, the communistic and socialistic world, or even the affluent atheistic societies which have arisen from the ashes of the Judeo-Christian world throughout Europe, America, and the rest of the western world.

The *world* in the Greek is often literally the *cosmos,* which means the "order" or the "adornment." The *world* is the order of things—the system, the way things operate (other than in the Kingdom of God). The cosmos is man organizing himself without God.

As a fish wouldn't realize what water is, so we do not realize the "order" around us until we are called out of it through the Gospel. Before I became born-again, all I ever knew were the ways of the world. Even as I grew to maturity, all of the understanding I gained was merely more and more worldly wisdom.

None of these things are consciously formed, humanly speaking, but there is a mind working behind and through the world, (i.e., the "prince of this world").

Thus, we are told the world hates Christ and will not glorify God. The world does not receive the Holy Spirit, for it doesn't know Him or Christ, neither does it have the love of the Father.

> If the world hate you, ye know that it hated me before it hated you. If ye were of the world, the world would love his own: but because ye are not of the world, but I have chosen you out of the world, therefore the world hateth you. (John 15:18-19)

Lying In the Power of the Wicked One

Another word often translated in the New Testament as *the world* is *aion,* which means "age." Galatians 1:4 tells us that Jesus delivered us from the evils of this present age (world).

We are explicitly commanded to "love not the world." In order to do this, we need to recognize that which is of this world so that we can separate ourselves from its evil influence.

> Love not the world, neither the things that are in the world. If any man love the world, the love of the Father is not in him. For all that is in the world, the lust of the flesh, and the lust of the eyes, and the pride of life, is not of the Father, but is of the world. And the world passeth away, and the lust thereof: but he that doeth the will of God abideth for ever. (1 John 2:15-17)

> [K]now ye not that the friendship of the world is enmity with God? whosoever therefore will be a friend of the world is the enemy of God. (James 4:4)

Here we learn that the "things that are in the world" are of a fallen value system consisting of three primary values:

- *The lust of the flesh*—This is the inordinate desire to experience things, everything, on our own terms, and to the exclusion of God.

- *The lust of the eyes*—This refers to the inordinate desire to have things, on our own terms, and to the exclusion of God.
- *The boastful pride of life*—This is the inordinate desire to be whoever we want to be, with no consideration for the will of God nor any acknowledgment of Him.

Remember the serpent tempted the first couple to eat the fruit so they would be as gods, "to know good and evil." What this meant is that they would be given the power to choose for themselves what good and evil are. They wouldn't need to rely on God or accept His Word; they themselves would decide for themselves what would be good . . . or evil.

This was the birth of the "order" (the world), and this was the commencement of "this present evil world"—an entire world of autonomous creatures, independent of the Creator, and on their own. The couple would cover themselves in a vain effort to ease the pain of their shame and sorrow. This is what it means to be worldly, to live independently of God on one's own terms.

The world, it has been said, is the *social organism of sin and evil* for it excludes the Father, the Son, and the Holy Spirit.

The true "god" of this world is Satan himself, and he holds the whole world in the power of wickedness and deceit. The world is deceived. Blind men (agents of Satan) are being used to guide other blind men to the pit of eternal destruction.

The "prince of this world" has a doctrine for every kind of man, a false religion to, at least, give a pseudo answer to the nagging spiritual nature of fallen men. He uses the false religions of this world to do so, and he especially uses that horrible counterfeit, false Christianity, to deceive millions of people into a false and unfounded satisfaction for their uneasy consciences.

All false religions are worldly and ultimately, they are demonic. They usually end up persecuting the true religion just as Cain slew Abel. For the present, "this is [their] hour, and the power of darkness" (Luke 22:53).

The world and its lusts are passing away. God has already passed a sentence of judgment upon it, and His attitude toward it is uncompromising. There will be no improving the world or making the world a better place.

> But the day of the Lord will come as a thief in the night; in which the heavens shall pass away with a great noise, and the elements shall melt with fervent heat, the earth also and the works that are therein shall be burned up. Seeing then that all these things shall be dissolved, what manner of persons ought ye to be in all holy conversation and godliness, Looking for and hasting unto the coming of the day of God, wherein the heavens being on fire

shall be dissolved, and the elements shall melt with fervent heat? Nevertheless we, according to his promise, look for new heavens and a new earth, wherein dwelleth righteousness. (2 Peter 3:10-13)

CHAPTER EIGHT

TEMPTATION: THE UNDERLYING RELIGIOUS PRINCIPLE

In Genesis 3 we see the temptation of the first Adam (along with his wife). There is much to learn in the account about the nature of the adversary, human psychology, and the power of well-crafted lies to seduce us.

In Matthew 4, we have another temptation narrative, that of the "last Adam." The Lord Jesus Christ had been baptized and affirmed by the very voice of God and anointed with the Spirit of God when He was led of the Spirit out into the wilderness. It was time to engage in spiritual conflict.

Jesus is tempted as a man and not in a garden of delights but, fittingly, in a harsh and unforgiving desert. Our Savior is alone, and all He has as an arsenal is His memory of Scripture. He has been fasting and in much prayer. At the point in the fast when the hunger would re-emerge with a vengeance, the Tempter came to Him.

Turn These Stones into Bread

THE TEMPTER SPOKE TO Jesus, and He knew it was the serpent's voice, which said:

> If thou be the Son of God, command that these stones be made bread. (Matthew 4:3)

The first temptation against Jesus had this in common with the original temptation—it had to do with food. We all need it for our sustenance. There is no question about that. Furthermore, a man fasting for forty days is greatly aware of his need for sustenance. The smooth stones in the various *wadis* with which the Judean wilderness teemed would actually resemble loaves of bread, especially after forty days of fasting.

But the temptation ran deeper, for He was being tempted to do something "out of Himself" concerning His need, to use the power which God had entrusted to Him: miraculously turn these stones into bread.

Underneath every temptation, no matter how seemingly mundane, a religious principle is being called into question. Far deeper issues are at stake.

Humanly speaking, the issue in this case is: would Jesus rely on the Father alone to feed Him in *His* time? Or should Jesus take matters into His own hands and use God's power to solve His own problem and meet His own need? Satan was calling on Jesus to take matters into His own hands and to prove to Himself that indeed He really *was* the Son of God.

Temptation

However, Jesus, the Son of God, was also "the last Adam" (1 Corinthians 15:45, 47) who came to redeem us. His grasp of Scripture had unique depth in that He came to fulfill it as the Living Word. In this case, there was already a scriptural similitude to Jesus' temptation other than the temptation of Adam and Eve in the garden. Jesus knew He was retracing the steps of the nation of Israel, for they too had been brought out into the wilderness to be tempted sorely, that they might learn one important lesson.

> And thou shalt remember all the way which the LORD thy God led thee these forty years in the wilderness, to humble thee, and to prove thee, to know what was in thine heart, whether thou wouldest keep his commandments, or no. And he humbled thee, and suffered thee to hunger, and fed thee with manna, which thou knewest not, neither did thy fathers know; *that he might make thee know that man doth not live by bread only, but by every word that proceedeth out of the mouth of the LORD doth man live.* (Deuteronomy 8:2-3; emphasis added)

The one great lesson intended in the wilderness was that man does not live by physical bread alone nor by anything temporal or material; education, entertainment, approval, the honor of our fellow men will all temporarily satisfy, but eventually fall short. We were made to be sustained by something much higher and purer.

Nothing the material world has to offer is adequate to satisfy our deepest longing, which happens to be spiritual.

We will never be able to live without communion with God Himself. Sadly, this remains impossible for us because of sin and alienation from God.

This is why it is not simply a matter of Jesus "using" the power entrusted to Him to turn those stones into bread by His own volition and impetus. Jesus was waiting for God to feed Him in the wilderness. He would not succumb to the temptation to turn those stones into bread on His own initiative.

What we see Jesus demonstrating for us is the importance of a full dependence on God for His leading and provisions. Jesus knew that God's Word *is* our true food and sustenance.

Thus, Jesus drew from the Scripture implanted in His heart, and in the midst of temptation spoke, "It is written . . ."

Why should the person who is in truth the eternal Word of God and the true Author and originator of all Scripture have to say, "It is written . . ."? Couldn't He legitimately say, "I command" or "I have spoken"? Why does He speak in the third person, "It is written . . ."?

The answer is that Jesus is being tempted as a man and not His own man but as a man under God, citing the Word of God as the authority. By saying, "It is written," He is invoking the authority above Himself as a man and standing underneath that authority in His conflict with the devil.

This is hugely significant to us in these modern days of ungrounded self-confidence. Today, the false spiritual warfare teaching actually encourages believers to do the very opposite of Jesus—to rail against Satan and the demons. Jude and Peter warn us against this practice:

> Likewise also these filthy dreamers defile the flesh, despise dominion, and speak evil of dignities. Yet Michael the archangel, when contending with the devil he disputed about the body of Moses, durst not bring against him a railing accusation, but said, The Lord rebuke thee. But these speak evil of those things which they know not: but what they know naturally, as brute beasts, in those things they corrupt themselves. (Jude 8-10)

Jesus does no such thing. Rather, He stands in His place as a man under God and under the very authority of the Scriptures and invokes those Scriptures in the very face of the devil. He knows what the temptation really is and that the underlying religious principle is at stake; the issue goes far beyond the mere satisfaction of a temporal hunger.

In response, He quotes the passage in Deuteronomy:

> [M]an doth not live by bread only, but by every word that proceedeth out of the mouth of the LORD. (Deuteronomy 8:3)

THE PINNACLE OF THE TEMPLE

> Then the devil taketh him up into the holy city, and setteth him on a pinnacle of the temple, And saith unto him, If thou be the Son of God, cast thyself down: for it is written, He shall give his angels charge concerning thee: and in their hands they shall bear thee up, lest at any time thou dash thy foot against a stone. Jesus said unto him, It

is written again, Thou shalt not tempt the Lord
thy God. (Matthew 4:5-7)

MUCH OF SPIRITUAL WARFARE is a matter of temptation. Satan is the tempter who seeks to provoke the children of God into denying Christ by succumbing to various temptations.

The temptation of Jesus yields deep insights into the nature of the adversary and of the spiritual warfare in which we find ourselves engaged.

Some aspects of the temptation of the Son of God were representative, as was the temptation of Adam. In the wilderness, Jesus passed the test which our first father failed. He overcame the devil for us as the "last Adam." Thank God, none of the redeemed will ever endure a temptation with so much at stake. Now in the temple, the Devil was making a mockery of the Word of God.

In a mysterious sense, the temptations of Jesus were real and the stakes were high; the salvation of us all was on the line. Christ is victor!

On the other hand, there is much to be gleaned regarding the "wiles of the devil" (Ephesians 6:11) and the way to victory in the spiritual warfare of the church.

The underlying issues of Jesus' temptations are manifold. For example: What was the Temple's true purpose? Satan would have Jesus draw attention to Himself in the house of prayer for all nations in order to begin His ministry by a dramatic exhibition of power and deliverance. The temptation was for signs and wonders and demonstrations of power, but it was not for that purpose that Jesus came.

TEMPTATION

This temptation was real and quite compelling when we take into account the messianic expectation of the popular rabbis and sages. Alfred Eidersheim (1825-1889) notes that there was a widely expected teaching that Messiah would perform just such a feat at His advent:

> In the Commentary just referred to . . . the placing of Messiah on the pinnacle of the Temple, so far from being of Satanic temptation, is said to mark the hour of deliverance, of Messianic proclamation, and of Gentile voluntary submission. Our Rabbis give this tradition: In the hour when King Messiah cometh, He standeth upon the roof of the Sanctuary, and proclaims to Israel, saying, Ye poor (suffering), the time of your redemption draweth nigh. And if ye believe, rejoice in My Light, which is risen upon you . . . Is. lx. 1 . . . upon you only . . . Is. lx. 2 . . . In that hour will the Holy One, blessed be His Name, make the Light of the Messiah and of Israel to shine forth; and all shall come to the Light of the King Messiah and of Israel, as it is written . . . Is. lx. 3 . . . And they shall come and lick the dust from under the feet of the King Messiah, as it is written, Is. xlix.[20]

On top of that, Satan added a Scripture:

> There shall no evil befall thee, neither shall any plague come nigh thy dwelling. For he shall give his angels charge over thee, to keep thee

in all thy ways. They shall bear thee up in their hands, lest thou dash thy foot against a stone. (Psalm 91:10-12)

The misuse of Scripture is a powerful device of Satan because believers (rightly) reverence Scripture; thus, it gives a false authority to many of Satan's twisted arguments. Satan and his agents "use" Scripture to deceive and seduce.

This is an important and profound revelation. Like Jesus, we use Scripture, rightly divided and applied, to counter Satan's proposals. John said to the "young men" that they were "strong, and the word of God" was in them and that they had "overcome the wicked one" (1 John 2:14).

Yet we must realize that Satan resorts to Scripture also—of course, always twisted, misapplied, and tortured. What we see in Matthew 4 is a religious argument between Satan and Jesus.

The 91st Psalm is a God-given promise of protection and provision for all who fear God and are written in the book of life. He really does appoint His angels to protect His people in their earthly sojourn. But is that promise a basis for any believer to do something self-seeking and reckless to force God's hand? Can any believer "use" a promise of God to obligate Him to act?

The sin is called *presumption*. All of God's promises are true. God is faithful. However, the promises are all fulfilled on His terms and at His initiative; He cannot be manipulated.

Hearkening back to the context of Deuteronomy, Jesus could see that the suggestion to forcefully and publicly fulfill the general messianic expectation, and to misuse the very Temple of the Lord for His own self-promotion, was a sinful snare. It was putting the Lord to the test, as Israel had done in the wilderness at Massah, when they demanded, "Is the LORD among us, or not?" (Exodus 17:7).

True reverence for Scripture—careful study of it in context, and the effort to grasp the whole picture in the text in the larger flow of Scripture, as well as prayerful dependence upon God, can save us from the sophisticated deception of the wicked one.

The whole concept of "using" Scripture—proof-texting, picking and choosing particular verses over others, or even the superstitious use of verses with little or no regard for actual context or for cross references—predisposes Christians to be open to deception.

To refute Satan's taunts to throw Himself off the Temple, Jesus again turns to Scripture, standing as a Son under the authority of God, His Father: "Ye shall not tempt the LORD your God" (Deuteronomy 6:16).

THE QUESTION OF WORSHIP

> Again, the devil taketh him up into an exceeding high mountain, and sheweth him all the kingdoms of the world, and the glory of them; And saith unto him, All these things will I give thee, if thou wilt fall down and worship me. Then saith Jesus unto him, Get thee hence, Satan: for it is written, Thou shalt worship the Lord thy God, and him only shalt thou serve. (Matthew 4:8-10)

WE CAN ONLY MARVEL at the vast powers temporarily granted to the devil in this account of the temptation of Jesus. Consider that Satan was able to transport Jesus to the very pinnacle of the Temple of God in the previous temptation. Was He taken there in a vision, trance, or perhaps a dream? Or was Jesus somehow actually physically transported by the adversary to the Temple in Jerusalem? We don't know for sure, but the experience was vivid and real.

Again, in this final temptation, Satan is able to show Jesus all of the kingdoms of this world and their glory. Then the adversary offered the kingdoms of this world to Jesus as if they were his to give. According to Luke's account, Satan was claiming that these kingdoms *were* his, having been given to him:

> And the devil said unto him, All this power will I give thee, and the glory of them: for that is delivered unto me; and to whomsoever I will I give it. (Luke 4:6)

Jesus didn't deny Satan's assertion.

Who is this malevolent being set against the church and against the Word of God? He is called the "prince of this world" twice in the Gospel of John; and Paul, by the Holy Spirit, refers to Satan as the "god of this world." John warns us that "the whole world lieth in wickedness." And Paul warns:

> For we wrestle not against flesh and blood, but against principalities, against powers, against the rulers of the darkness of this world,

against spiritual wickedness in high places. (Ephesians 6:12)

This is why the present age has been called "this present evil world" and "the evil day."

All of the influences and institutions of this world—education, religion, entertainment, information sources, the opinion shapers, molders of minds, leadership in law, commerce, government, and even medicine—have come under the power of, and are at the service of, the prince of this world.

The Apocalypse tells us that soon "the kingdoms of this world" shall become "the kingdoms of our Lord, and of his Christ" (Revelation 11:15). This is one of the final turns of events of the eschaton,* but it necessitates Jesus offering Himself as a sacrifice for our sins, suffering, dying, and being raised from the dead, thus inaugurating the *church age*.

But Satan offered Jesus a much easier path to glory at the cost of a momentary compromise. Satan presented Jesus with a classic ends/means situation. Here was an easier way to attain His goal—a way without the humiliation and sufferings of the Cross.

We gain insight into the core issue of spiritual warfare in this story. We see what issues all meld into the real conflict raging for the souls of men and women: worship. Man was made to worship, and he *will* worship. But worship is

---

* Eschaton: (literally) the last; used in theology to refer to the world's state during the posthistoric era of God's overt (apocalyptic) reign, immediately preceding the end of the world (https://www.yourdictionary.com/eschaton).

exclusive; we were created to worship God alone. Jesus gave clear direction on this when He stated:

> Thou shalt love the Lord thy God with all thy heart, and with all thy soul, and with all thy mind. (Matthew 22:37)

Only God is worthy of all our affections. He who made us, completes us. To worship anything that is less than God is the very essence of sin. We fell as a race because we "knew God" but "glorified him not as God" (Romans 1:21). This is the fountainhead of our corruption.

Satan has set himself as the rival to God for the affections of mankind. All false worship is, in fact, Satan worship. The devil craves and demands worship. He has the entire world of unbelieving men and women in deception worshipping manmade idols, false gods such as Allah or Buddha, or, in the secular world, technology and the achievements of modern men.

The Lord Jesus again prevailed, but not in Himself, humanly speaking. Jesus overcame the very real and powerful temptation to worship Satan by invoking the Word of God. "It is written . . ."

There in the wilderness, Jesus proclaimed to His adversary: "Thou shalt worship the Lord thy God, and him only shalt thou serve."

Perhaps the greatest and final test for humanity is coming rapidly, when all men will be required to wear a mark on their hand or forehead if they want to buy, sell, or trade. Such a "mark" in the form of a tiny chip has already been introduced in this "smart planet" we have created by our technology. According to a NPR article, thousands of Swedish citizens have now had this smart chip inserted into the hand:

> Technology continues to get closer and closer to our bodies, from the phones in our pockets to the smartwatches on our wrists. Now, for some people, it's getting under their skin.
>
> In Sweden, a country rich with technological advancement, thousands have had microchips inserted into their hands.
>
> The chips are designed to speed up users' daily routines and make their lives more convenient—accessing their homes, offices and gyms is as easy as swiping their hands against digital readers. . . .
>
> So many Swedes are lining up to get the microchips that the country's main chipping company says it can't keep up with the number of requests.[21]

The world is being conditioned and prepared to receive "the mark of the beast" (Revelation 19:20). When that day comes, it will just seem to be the next step in the decades-long shift from cash and checks to digitalized commerce. There will be so many obvious practical reasons for this; it will seem retrograde to resist it.

In the evaluation of God, however, participation in the mark will be considered an unforgivable act of worship. It will be the final act of man's defiance and defection from God.

Following the Gospel in these last days will have its own unique challenges in that it will come as a call to worship the true God and to realize the beast system is more than political or economic; it is a system of false worship.

> Saying with a loud voice, Fear God, and give glory to him; for the hour of his judgment is come: and worship him that made heaven, and earth, and the sea, and the fountains of waters. And there followed another angel, saying, Babylon is fallen, is fallen, that great city, because she made all nations drink of the wine of the wrath of her fornication. And the third angel followed them, saying with a loud voice, If any man worship the beast and his image, and receive his mark in his forehead, or in his hand, The same shall drink of the wine of the wrath of God, which is poured out without mixture into the cup of his indignation; and he shall be tormented with fire and brimstone in the presence of the holy angels, and in the presence of the Lamb: And the smoke of their torment ascendeth up for ever and ever: and they have no rest day nor night, who worship the beast and his image, and whosoever receiveth the mark of his name. (Revelation 14:7-11)

CHAPTER NINE

WHO DO THE KINGS OF THE EARTH SERVE?

> Why do the heathen rage, and the people imagine a vain thing? The kings of the earth set themselves, and the rulers take counsel together, against the Lord, and against his anointed, saying, Let us break their bands asunder, and cast away their cords from us. He that sitteth in the heavens shall laugh: the Lord shall have them in derision. (Psalm 2:1-4)

A RULING ELITE HAS emerged in this postmodern "progressive" world which is very openly waging war with the God of the Bible and of Christ.

The second Psalm is a prophecy of these men, calling them "the kings of the earth" and their "rulers."

It is important to note at this point that this description is not limited to political figures, presidents, prime ministers, or leaders. The kings of the earth and their rulers refer to political and governmental figures indeed, but it is not limited to them. What the Psalm is referring to is what we would call the "ruling elite" in all areas of influence in society. These men and women are the leaders in education, religion, entertainment, banking and finance, economics, the cultural movers and shakers, the shapers of men's opinions, the gatekeepers in modern life.

The second Psalm takes on special prophetic significance in referring to these "elites" as "the kings of the Earth" who will take counsel together against the Lord and His Christ.

Where have they taken this counsel? How have so many of our elites come to an anti-Christian consensus? How did the Judeo-Christian world elite transform into the secular, atheistic elite that it is now?

It turns out they received what has been in the works for centuries: the anti-God and anti-Christ counsel that is propagated in our institutions of higher education.

The Psalmist also warns us that the kings of the earth and their rulers are carrying out their counsel against the Lord and His Christ by conducting an ongoing "liberation movement"—breaking Judeo/Christian society away from all of the former structures and constructs which once formed Western society.

The kings of the earth and their rulers have been on a long march through every one of our institutions, tearing down or plucking out by the roots the moral and spiritual foundational supports of our culture: the value of life, the meaning of humanity, the definition of marriage, Judeo/Christian sexuality, the differences between genders. They destroy the unity of society by agitating and exploiting disaffected identity groups. And this is not just happening in secular institutions; an increasing number of Christian colleges and seminaries are embracing the elements of this tearing down process.

These cultural elites have foisted upon the people of the West a philosophy of Nihilism. This philosophy has been evolving in academia and has seeped into the mainstream of our society through the media, entertainment, and education in many forms. It is currently expressed in multiculturalism.

Multiculturalism seemingly started out as a celebration of the "diversity" of humanity and the recognition of the contributions of cultures other than Western. This philosophy evolved into the manifestly erroneous idea that all cultures are in fact equal in value, and that any assertions of cultural superiority in any area (by Westerners) is proof of bigotry.

The end point of the evolution of this errant philosophy (perhaps it was the goal all along) is that all cultures (i.e., third world, African tribal, Islamic, Buddhist, Hindu, Communist, etc.) are superior to classical Western culture. While all men are equal in worth and value, to say all cultures are equal in value and validity is erroneous.

Western culture, the most successful, humane, reasonable, liberating, productive, just, humanly-elevating, merciful civilization the world has ever seen, is now portrayed as racist, exploitive, bigoted, greedy, and murderous. The "left" has succeeded in slandering the West in spite of the manifest success of the culture. The youth of our culture, especially, have been indoctrinated into this diabolical lie.

I believe the reason for this "vain imagination" is because Western civilization has its roots in Judeo-Christianity.

Thus, the cultural flavor of the day—in spite of its manifest misogyny, brutality, hatred, open bigotry, blood lust, and fervent murderous expansionism—is Islam.

In the face of universal Islamic "rape waves," murder, assault, terrorism in astonishing magnitude, our cultural elites not only insist upon the "peacefulness of Islam" but seek to engorge our formerly civil and orderly societies with millions of Muslims who openly hate those who do not believe Allah to be God.

This was all prophesied in the second Psalm.

The kings of the earth theme in end-times predictions is in both Old and New Testaments.

For example, Isaiah tells us that one of the reasons for the final devastating judgments coming on the Earth is that the kings of the earth have broken the "everlasting covenant."

> The earth also is defiled under the inhabitants thereof; because they have transgressed the laws, changed the ordinance, broken the everlasting covenant . . . And it shall come to pass in that day, that the LORD shall punish the host of the high ones that are on high, and the kings of the earth upon the earth. (Isaiah 24:5, 21)

The hosts on high refers to the judgment of the principalities, powers, and rulers of the darkness of this age (i.e., the demonic hierarchy), while the kings of the Earth refers to the human ruling elite.

WHO DO THE KINGS OF THE EARTH SERVE?

The Lord will soon punish them for what they have made of this world. The kings of the earth have participated in a worldwide rebellion against the Lord and His Christ.

Psalm 48 tells us that their rebellion also involves resistance to God's plan for Jerusalem.

> Great is the LORD, and greatly to be praised in the city of our God, in the mountain of his holiness. Beautiful for situation, the joy of the whole earth, is mount Zion, on the sides of the north, the city of the great King. God is known in her palaces for a refuge. For, lo, the kings were assembled, they passed by together. They saw it, and so they marvelled; they were troubled, and hasted away. Fear took hold upon them there, and pain, as of a woman in travail. (Psalm 48:1-6)

The kings of the earth are already assembling against Jerusalem. The U.N. is nearly unanimous in its condemnation of Israel's possession of Jerusalem, and in 2017, Pope Francis prayed openly that Jerusalem would remain divided.[22] The same Pope announced himself at the 70th U.N. General Assembly in 2015 by saying he had come, "In my own name, and that of the entire Catholic community."[23]

Make no mistake, Pope Francis is one of the powerful "kings of the earth" who have taken sides against the Lord and His Christ.

On February 5, 2018, Pope Francis met with Turkey president, Recep Tayyip Erdogan at the Vatican. The two also met together in 2014 when the Pope visited Erdogan in Turkey. Erdogan has pledged to unite the Muslim world to retake Israel and Jerusalem. Why would the head of the Catholic Church meet with an avowed Islamist? On both visits, news reports around the world stated that the two men would be discussing "Islamophobia" and Israel. Erdogan wanted to commend the Pope for his resistance to Trump's call for Jerusalem to be the capital of Israel.

Pope Francis with Recep Tayyip Erdogan of Turkey at the Turkish presidential palace in 2014

Who Do the Kings of the Earth Serve?

The U.N. voted almost entirely to renounce Jewish claims to Jerusalem. This is in direct defiance to God Himself and will soon bring the final judgment. But the kings of the earth are currently all being led by Satan and his evil spirits, though in many cases, they do not realize it.

Revelation 16 tells us that demons like frogs will come out of the Antichrist's mouth to bring all of the kings of the earth into war.

> And I saw three unclean spirits like frogs come out of the mouth of the dragon, and out of the mouth of the beast, and out of the mouth of the false prophet. For they are the spirits of devils, working miracles, which go forth unto the kings of the earth and of the whole world, to gather them to the battle of that great day of God Almighty. (Revelation 16:13-14)

When Jesus actually returns, the Beast, the kings of the Earth, and their armies will step out of the shadow to resist Him personally:

> And I saw the beast, and the kings of the earth, and their armies, gathered together to make war against him that sat on the horse, and against his army. (Revelation 19:19)

But they will not be able to face the Lamb of God in His full wrath:

> And the kings of the earth, and the great men, and the rich men, and the chief captains, and the mighty men, and every bondman, and every free man, hid themselves in the dens and in the rocks of the mountains; And said to the mountains and rocks, Fall on us, and hide us from the face of him that sitteth on the throne, and from the wrath of the Lamb: For the great day of his wrath is come; and who shall be able to stand? (Revelation 6:15-17)

These "ruling elite" are among the tools Satan employs to make war against the saints.

CHAPTER TEN

THE SERPENT AND THE DRAGON

And there appeared a great wonder in heaven; a woman clothed with the sun, and the moon under her feet, and upon her head a crown of twelve stars: And she being with child cried, travailing in birth, and pained to be delivered. And there appeared another wonder in heaven; and behold a great red dragon, having seven heads and ten horns, and seven crowns upon his heads. And his tail drew the third part of the stars of heaven, and did cast them to the earth: and the dragon stood before the woman which was ready to be delivered, for to devour her child as soon as it was born. (Revelation 12:1-4)

THE ENEMY OF GOD and of man comes to us either as a serpent or a dragon. We have commented on the subtlety of the serpent in an earlier chapter. We have seen that some of his tactics have included: his seduction of our first parents, the use of questions filled with evil, implied accusations against God, and the centuries of crafting and disseminating various soul-destroying philosophies, and false "knowledge" calculated to estrange men from the Creator and damn them forever.

This is the subtle side of the devil.

Subtlety is necessary when one is on the outside trying to gain access, or to seduce in order to gain something from the unsuspecting. Serpents slither and whisper. They insinuate and crouch in their coils until they have the opportunity to strike.

But as the vision of Revelation 12 shows us, the devil is both a serpent and a dragon, depending on the situation.

In a nutshell, Revelation 12 is the corresponding chapter to Genesis 3.

What do we see in Genesis 3? A woman, a man, a serpent, and the promise of a virgin-born Deliverer, "the Seed of the woman."

By Revelation 12, the woman is clothed and pregnant, writhing in labor. The "Seed of the woman" has come and has been taken up into Heaven (v. 5). The serpent has become a great red dragon with seven heads, ten horns, and seven crowns upon his head. He has vast political power and has won many victories.

What is the essence of this mysterious symbolism, revealed by the Holy Spirit?

THE SERPENT AND THE DRAGON

In apocalyptic imagery, a woman is often a symbol for a spiritual body. Thus, faithful Israel is often referred to as "the daughter of Zion":

> Rejoice greatly, O daughter of Zion; shout, O daughter of Jerusalem: behold, thy King cometh unto thee: he is just, and having salvation; lowly, and riding upon an ass, and upon a colt the foal of an ass. (Zechariah 9:9)

Unfaithful or backslidden Israel is likened unto a harlot in prophetic imagery:

> How is the faithful city become an harlot! it was full of judgment; righteousness lodged in it; but now murderers. (Isaiah 1:21)

In the New Testament also, the believing church is called "the elect lady" (2 John 1:1) and "the bride" of Christ (Revelation 21:9). Also, it says:

> Let us be glad and rejoice, and give honour to him: for the marriage of the Lamb is come, and his wife hath made herself ready. (Revelation 19:7)

> For I am jealous over you with godly jealousy: for I have espoused you to one husband, that I may present you as a chaste virgin to Christ. (2 Corinthians 11:2)

The woman in the vision is generally a picture of the true people of God. They wait for Him, and believe in Him, and are willing to bear all suffering for His truth. On one level, this is the meaning of the woman.

There is also a more specific identification to this woman, for often apocalyptic visions have layers of meaning. The woman clothed in the sun, moon, and the stars as depicted in the dream of Joseph, represents the sun, moon, and stars as Jacob, Leah, and the twelve sons of Israel. Therefore the woman is Israel. She is the specific woman which the serpent hates and has often tried to destroy.

Her Seed, the Messiah, defeated the serpent in battle, and it is He who shall soon come to "rule all nations with a rod of iron" (Revelation 12:5). The child taken up is the Lord Jesus Christ, who came, died, rose again, and will soon return to rule the nations with a rod of iron.

The great red dragon is also identified in the 12th chapter of Revelation:

> And the great dragon was cast out, that old serpent, called the Devil, and Satan, which deceiveth the whole world: he was cast out into the earth, and his angels were cast out with him. (Revelation 12:9)

Literally, the text calls him, "that serpent of old." *He is the same person as the one who lured Adam and Eve to their spiritual suicide in the garden.* That serpent is also a dragon.

In areas of the world where there is a strong Judeo-Christian influence, Satan is making war on saints, and basically, on mankind in general, as the serpent. He employs

THE SERPENT AND THE DRAGON

lies, subtlety, the use of heresy, vain imaginations, reasonings and philosophies, and a flood of deception.

However, where there is little or no Judeo-Christian influence, Satan reveals himself as the persecutor of God's saints, the dragon who openly devours.

In Revelation 12, the dragon waits for the woman (Israel), who is pregnant, to bring forth the Seed of the woman (the Messiah). This was the meaning behind the attempts of Pharaoh to take Abraham's wife, and Isaac's wife, and the Pharaoh's attempt to kill Hebrew children, and Queen Athaliah's attempt to win over the children of the son of David. The dragon was behind all of this turmoil across the centuries to Herod who slew the babes at Bethlehem.

> [A]nd the dragon stood before the woman which was ready to be delivered, for to devour her child as soon as it was born. (Revelation 12:4)

By this time, no subtlety was necessary. The dragon was able to be open about his malice and "to steal, and to kill, and to destroy" (John 10:10), as Jesus told us he would.

The dragon's power is vast and fearful, but he still must serve God's purposes just as Judas did. He is allowed to be the serpent and the dragon, yet his malice in the war he makes on the saints fulfills God's glorious purposes.

> Therefore rejoice, ye heavens, and ye that dwell in them. Woe to the inhabiters of the earth and of the sea! for the devil is come down unto you, having great wrath, because he knoweth that he hath but a short time. And when the dragon saw

> that he was cast unto the earth, he persecuted
> the woman which brought forth the man child.
> (Revelation 12:12-13)

The dragon knows his time is limited. He will soon be cast to the Earth, and this will usher in a greater persecution of Israel and the saints than has ever been seen before. Already in the Muslim world, as well as in the Hindu and Buddhist worlds, the saints have been suffering a severe persecution by the dragon.

We know why he would attack the true church; they bear witness to the truth of God in the face of the Lie, which is being received and accepted throughout the world.

But why does the dragon yet seek to destroy the woman, the children of Israel? He failed in his attempt to wipe out the "Seed of the woman"; the Man-Child has come and done His saving work and has ascended to Heaven. Certainly Israel is at present under the deception of the dragon, as are all the nations. Why is she a threat to the dragon?

The dragon knows that God's promises are invested in the woman. He has said she will endure forever and that He would place them back in the land and in one day, would save the entire nation. If Israel could be wiped out before any of this is fulfilled, God would have failed to keep His Word.

> Thus saith the LORD, which giveth the sun for a
> light by day, and the ordinances of the moon and
> of the stars for a light by night, which divideth
> the sea when the waves thereof roar; The LORD
> of hosts is his name: If those ordinances depart
> from before me, saith the LORD, then the seed

of Israel also shall cease from being a nation before
me for ever. Thus saith the LORD; If heaven
above can be measured, and the foundations of
the earth searched out beneath, I will also cast off
all the seed of Israel for all that they have done,
saith the LORD. (Jeremiah 31:35-37)

In this way, the woman is still pregnant and is in labor pain. She has already borne the pain and reproach and trial and privilege of bringing the Scriptures into the world and being the site of the only true worship on Earth; and she has been the receptacle nation of the Seed of the woman. Satan has failed to halt any of these things.

Before the physical kingdom of God (i.e., when Christ returns to rule) will commence, Israel, as a whole nation, will repent, recognizing Jesus as her Messiah. This is a key point in the role the Jews will have in the last days—a role that is immensely significant, contrary to the teaching of replacement theology. On the prophetic scale, this time is referred to in the Book of Revelation as the great tribulation and the time of Jacob's trouble. God is pressing Israel to repent, and Satan seeks to destroy her through the kings of the Earth. God told her:

> I will go and return to my place, till they
> acknowledge their offence, and seek my face:
> in their affliction they will seek me early.
> (Hosea 5:15)

> And the serpent cast out of his mouth water as
> a flood after the woman, that he might cause

her to be carried away of the flood. And the earth helped the woman, and the earth opened her mouth, and swallowed up the flood which the dragon cast out of his mouth. And the dragon was wroth with the woman, and went to make war with the remnant of her seed, which keep the commandments of God, and have the testimony of Jesus Christ. (Revelation 12:15-17)

CHAPTER ELEVEN

THE WARFARE IS CONFESSIONAL

> And when they bring you unto the synagogues, and unto magistrates, and powers, take ye no thought how or what thing ye shall answer, or what ye shall say: For the Holy Ghost shall teach you in the same hour what ye ought to say. (Luke 12:11-12)

NOTICE THAT JESUS SAYS "*when* they bring you before" not *if* they bring you before.

Sooner or later, every Christian, on some level, will be called upon to make the good confession. The setting is never a favorable one; it will range from either mildly hostile to absolutely death-dealing hatred, but we are being and will be called upon to make our confession.

We don't have to rehearse our confession. The Holy Spirit will give us what to say when we are called up before various human tribunals. It will just come out of us naturally, this good confession of truth, in the day of our own trial.

This blessed promise of the Holy Spirit's help presupposes that we are in a vigorous spiritual war and that all of us are participants, wittingly or unwittingly.

The Spirit will help us, whether we are brought to account in the synagogue or before a secular judge or in the presence of hostile friends and relatives or perhaps at human resource offices at work. We will know what to say and have the power to say it boldly.

The further assumption of this promise of the Lord Jesus is that the nature of the battle in the spiritual realm is in large part confessional. The Holy Spirit will empower us to confess, to affirm the truth of God even in the face of hostility. God wants a witness—people who will stand up and bear witness to the truth in *the day of the Lie.*

This is why we, the church, remain in this world which is so hostile to Christ.

> But ye shall receive power, after that the Holy Ghost is come upon you: and ye shall be witnesses unto me both in Jerusalem, and in all Judaea, and in Samaria, and unto the uttermost part of the earth. (Acts 1:8)

It so happens that in the day in which we now live, the lie of Satan is the prevailing wisdom, embraced by virtually the entire earth. "[T]he whole world lieth in wickedness" (1 John 5:19).

Spiritual warfare includes both exposure of error and affirming the truth in the day of the Lie.

The Warfare is Confessional

But the promise of Luke 12:12, about what to expect when called upon to testify before hostile authorities, also presupposes the faithful witnesses have saturated themselves with biblical truth beforehand. In this brief passage, Jesus is teaching us how to prepare for spiritual warfare.

> In the mean time, when there were gathered together an innumerable multitude of people, insomuch that they trode one upon another, he began to say unto his disciples first of all, Beware ye of the leaven of the Pharisees, which is hypocrisy. (Luke 12:1)

First of all, some issues have to be settled in our own hearts—

> Jesus would have us beware of the influence, inside of us, of hypocrisy.

WHAT DOES *HYPOCRISY* MEAN? To practice hypocrisy, one has to pretend to be what one is not, or to pretend not to be what one is. The spiritual warfare we are already engaged in demands that we root out pretense in every form. Away with trying to be anything anymore, whether it be trying to be a "cool Christian," or a "relevant Christian," or to be seen as a "loving and nonjudgmental Christian" in comparison with the rest of the church. Away with all pretense! It is time to make a new commitment to be genuine.

A genuine person is not pretending. He is able to face himself and to be known by others as he really is—nothing more and nothing less.

The only one who is ready for the Holy Spirit to give him the power to make the "good confession" without rehearsal is the one who has already broken off with hypocrisy. He is the one who needs not "rehearse" anything in that hour because he can be himself (a self that is truly reliant on the Lord and is so influenced with the Word of God buried in his heart), which is the most convincing testimony. God will give him wisdom in his speech in that very hour.

After all, Jesus teaches us, hypocrisy is shortsighted, because sooner or later everything is going to be seen for what it truly is.

> For there is nothing covered, that shall not be revealed; neither hid, that shall not be known. Therefore whatsoever ye have spoken in darkness shall be heard in the light; and that which ye have spoken in the ear in closets shall be proclaimed upon the housetops. (Luke 12:2-3)

> Next, Jesus would have us decide once and for all, who it is that we truly fear.

> And I say unto you my friends, Be not afraid of them that kill the body, and after that have

> no more that they can do. But I will forewarn you whom ye shall fear: Fear him, which after he hath killed hath power to cast into hell; yea, I say unto you, Fear him. (Luke 12:4-5)

THE REAL SPIRITUAL WARFARE demands that we figure out who we are going to ultimately fear. Remember that fear in this sense is not limited to dread, angst, or fright; fear also refers to regard. To which audience do you play? Whom do you fear most, God or man? What can man do to you, beyond death?

The one who settles this issue of fear doesn't need to rehearse what he is going to say when he is called up to make the good confession. He knows who it is that he answers to, fears, and regards. He says God has power to cast body and soul into Hell, whereas all man can do is kill the body. Though this sounds gruesome, Jesus goes on to assure us that it is all right to fear God, for He is good, righteous, kind, and attentive to us.

> Are not five sparrows sold for two farthings, and not one of them is forgotten before God? But even the very hairs of your head are all numbered. Fear not therefore: ye are of more value than many sparrows. (Luke 12:6-7)

We can only fear one master; we cannot have dual fear.

> Finally, we have to really know what it means to confess Jesus before men, for the spiritual warfare is confessional.

> Also I say unto you, Whosoever shall confess me before men, him shall the Son of man also confess before the angels of God: But he that denieth me before men shall be denied before the angels of God. (Luke 12:8-9)

WHAT DOES IT MEAN to confess Christ before men? What does it mean to deny Christ?

A very basic and intuitive understanding of this Scripture would say that if a Christian is captured by atheists or other agents of antichrist and demanded, "Deny Christ or die!," to confess Christ would be to admit you are Christian, even if it costs you your life. We would all hope that in that moment, we would confess Christ and *love not our lives even unto death* as countless martyrs through the centuries have done.

This is a true and a valid understanding of this verse, but not a complete understanding of it.

Confessing Christ is not limited to merely admitting to being a Christian. To confess Christ is to identify with all that Christ stands for, represents, and has taught.

It is confession and not *profession*. Confessing Christ presupposes that to do so would be to expose the soul and possibly the body to difficulty and opposition. In our setting here in the West, it is not enough merely to say "I am a Christian"; there is little or no danger in that because the word *Christian* has undergone radical broadening to the point that it means little or nothing.

Remember that we live in the day of the lie, and each of us will be called upon to confess to the truth in various settings. Confessing Christ means to confess the *truth* of Christ.

Truth, even the truth of Christ and the Gospel, is vast. We must ask ourselves: which truth?

The answer is, whichever truth the spirit of antichrist is currently contesting, distorting, and outright denying.

In the 1500s and earlier, the truth of justification by faith was being denied. Thus, the warfare was carried forward by the reformers who re-emphasized this vital truth, even in the face of persecution by the organized church with its power to burn whom it deemed heretics at the stake.

What truths are being contested today? Confessing Christians today are in a battle of multi-level attacks. Biblical teachings on marriage, sex, gender, and homosexuality are being assaulted in the face of the rapidly changing worldly consensus. From within, confessing Christians are being challenged on essentials of the faith such as the atonement, the deity of Christ, the Trinity, and the validity of the Bible. Christians who do stand for and confess these truths are often ostracized, ridiculed, and marginalized, both in the secular media and much of mainstream Christian leadership. This is the spiritual warfare.

If the Lord would have a people who would confess Christ in the day of the Lie, what is the other side of the war?

Satan would pressure Christians to not only shut our mouths about the teachings of Christ, he would also pressure us with incredible force to confess that which we know in our hearts isn't true at all.

CHAPTER TWELVE

HOW PEOPLE DENY CHRIST (WITHOUT REALIZING IT)

> Also I say unto you, Whosoever shall confess me before men, him shall the Son of man also confess before the angels of God: But he that denieth me before men shall be denied before the angels of God. And whosoever shall speak a word against the Son of man, it shall be forgiven him: but unto him that blasphemeth against the Holy Ghost it shall not be forgiven. And when they bring you unto the synagogues, and unto magistrates, and powers, take ye no thought how or what thing ye shall answer, or what ye shall say: For the Holy Ghost shall teach you in the same hour what ye ought to say. (Luke 12:8-12)

WE HAVE BEEN MAKING the point that true spiritual warfare has a confessional component. We live in the day and age of Satan's lie. It is the conventional wisdom, accepted and approved by virtually the entire world.

As described in the previous chapter, God would have a people who live as witnesses to the truth. But truth is a vast and broad concept that while the primary thrust of the church is to witness to the Gospel, we need to be witnesses to the truths of God that are currently being undermined by the spirit of the age.

Though evolutionary thought would have us believe that we can live "just like the animals," the Bible reveals that God created us in His image to be moral agents of His righteousness.

In a day of the lie of "gay marriage" God would have a people who will bear witness to the Christian revelation of marriage, gender, family, and chastity.

To make the good confession presupposes that to do so would expose the soul and perhaps even the body to various levels of difficulty. Usually we are called upon to do so in hostile environments.

But the other side of this war, Satan, and the spirit of antichrist which is in the world, would not only shut our mouths from confessing the truth of Jesus, he would go further. In this warfare, the devil wants to pressure us to confess to what we know very well is an out and out lie.

This is the way he would have us to deny Christ, not that we would deny that we are Christian, but when we are called upon to stand up and confess to the truth of the teachings of Christ on any given element (which the world is denying), will we cave under pressure and in some cases make the bad confession?

I wrote an article about a remarkable case of this reality I saw one evening. It was a small (but large) skirmish in the very real spiritual war for the souls of men. The following is from the article which was called "How They Deny Jesus":

> I happened upon an airing of a Larry King show, in which two evangelical preachers and a noted evangelical pop musician were the guests. The musician, a young woman, had become noted for coming out as a lesbian yet wanting to continue in her "music ministry," to which she testified that there was much popular support.
>
> One of the evangelical pastors compassionately urged her to repent, assuring her of the prospect of God's forgiveness for all sins, citing Scripture against the sin as well as promises of God's love. This was indeed a faithful witness of the truth.
>
> He did this over the objections of Larry King, who obviously took the worldly position on the subject, treating lesbianism as a valid lifestyle and those who objected to it as bigots and haters. He accused the faithful pastor of being a "homophobe" and inferred he was a hypocrite and was similar to those in the fifties who would have objected to interracial marriage.
>
> Larry stood as we would expect, an avid proponent of the spirit of this age. He forced the good pastor to pay for the truth that he had espoused. So also did the young musician, who

laughed and mocked the pastor's attempt to call her on her sin and to bring her to repentance.

But the other pastor, a well-known evangelical, in fact a former head of the National Association of Evangelicals, sat by until Larry King asked him what he thought of the issue.

He turned to the faithful shepherd and said, "Remember Pastor, the only thing Jesus ever condemned anyone for was for judging others and telling them they are wrong!" At that moment, the young musician smiled, Larry King beamed, and I have no doubt that many in the listening audience appreciated the words of the second pastor.

It is as if they were all saying, "Here is someone who 'gets it,' unlike those obnoxious evangelical haters such as the first pastor. The second pastor is compassionate, understanding, humane, and non-judgmental—our kind of pastor. If only all Christians were as loving as this one."

But at that moment, I believe the Holy Spirit spoke to me and said, "Do you see what he just did? That man just gained the world." No, he didn't become rich and famous or better looking or more popular. That is not what "gaining the world" means in the teaching of Jesus.

How People Deny Christ

For just a sliver of the approval of a misguided pop singer in rebellion to God and the applause of a depraved, godless television personality, Larry King, and his audience, the second pastor in effect denied the biblical teaching on marriage and sexuality and sided with unbelievers against a faithful witness of Jesus. That was what he was willing to exchange for the chance to look "compassionate" before a television and radio audience. That was the price he was willing to pay.

The second preacher was willing to look good at the expense of his more faithful brother, who was being accused of being a "hater" by King, the young lesbian, and by inference, himself, when he chided the preacher for judging. This is the very way that many "shall betray one another" (Matthew 24:10) as our Lord warned us would be a characteristic of the last days.

That was what he was willing to "exchange for his soul." The man may have gained the world, but he lost part of his soul. Do you see what I mean by referring to constant transactions? In little or big ways, all of us are being put in that position almost every day, even if we don't realize it.[24]

Every day, in thousands of ways, such skirmishes are being fought, as Satan seeks to pressure people to confess what (they know) is not true. The *phenomenon* of "political correctness" is not a mere childish fad, it is spiritual warfare. The corruption of our very language and the pressure to go along with the godless consensus is by satanic design a way to brainwash and change people and to further the Lie.

There are many like the pastor in the story I just shared who betray the brethren and the faith. That pastor lost something of his soul, becoming a spiritual "prisoner of war" by denying the well-known teaching of Jesus on the subject of gender, marriage, and human sexuality, not recognizing the true nature of the battlefield.

But if you would have asked him, he would gladly have told you he was a Christian.

At the same time, there is a remnant of believers like the faithful pastor in the story, unashamed of the teaching of Jesus, ready to bear the reproach and humbly confess to it even in the face of ridicule and hostility. He overcame the devil by the very word of his testimony; he made the good confession and overcame.

The pressure in these days to succumb to the various lies is intense; all are part of the same big Lie. And we will be called upon again in the days ahead.

CHAPTER THIRTEEN

HOW WE WIN BY LOSING

And he shall speak great words against the most High, and shall wear out the saints of the most High, and think to change times and laws: and they shall be given into his hand until a time and times and the dividing of time. (Daniel 7:25)

And such as do wickedly against the covenant shall he corrupt by flatteries: but the people that do know their God shall be strong, and do exploits. And they that understand among the people shall instruct many: yet they shall fall by the sword, and by flame, by captivity, and by spoil, many days. Now when they shall fall, they shall be holpen with a little help: but many shall cleave to them with flatteries. And some of them of understanding shall fall, to try them, and to purge, and to make them white, even to

the time of the end: because it is yet for a time
appointed. (Daniel 11:32-35)

WHY DOES GOD PUT His people in situations where Satan makes war against the saints and overcomes them? How do martyrdom and persecution serve God's holy purposes?

Perhaps, it is a case, like the Cross of Jesus, where we win by losing.

Had the princes of this age known, they would not have crucified the Lord of Glory who brought redemption to the world.

Time and again, the people of the present age languish under the damning lie of Satan. In our own age, unbelief and cynicism rage, mocking everything holy, desecrating the sacred, ridiculing that remnant which does believe. Even the practitioners of the true faith are tempted to falter and fail as their leaders and pastors, Christian publishing houses, Christian media, and so-called Christian education accommodate the Lie on varying levels.

How can the thick veil of unbelief and sin-jaded hardness of heart ever be penetrated?

When truth and faith are nearly dead and the sacred is mocked, ridiculed, and twisted, and when the remnant itself is nearly as jaded as the people they claim to want to reach, God uses extreme measures.

What would cause people to see the Christian Gospel has gravitas and is true? Would it be when God causes people to be put in situations where to identify with it would cost them something, maybe everything, and letting the whole world see it.

How We Win by Losing

Remember John Lennon's anthem to atheism, the God-rejecting song, "Imagine" which tells us to imagine a world without Heaven, Hell, religion, and basically God. We now live in such a sad, pathetic world, crafted by socialist- and marxist-leaning leaders—a *progressive* movement inspired by Satan himself in which death is exalted. Think about it: be it evolution, homosexuality, transgenderism, abortion, suicide, occultism, sexual abuse and sex trafficking, violent video games and movies, they all lead to death, not life. What a sick, nihilistic world of people living for the present day and only to fulfill their own pleasures. I can't think of a more depressing and empty world. No wonder so many are living for entertainment, or on various legal and illegal drugs, or seeking to sate themselves in sex or novel foods.

We live in the day of which Paul warned where people have become lovers of themselves and lovers of pleasure, with no God. They don't believe in anything but the self and the now. They have scoffed at and dismissed the *old rugged Cross* while trying to fill the emptiness with other "values."

Suddenly, people hear about two bakers who lose their business and are subject to great ridicule and loss because they wouldn't cater a gay wedding.[25] Or they see the plight of a clerk in Kentucky who endured ridicule, abuse, and even some jail time because she wouldn't distribute marriage licenses to homosexual couples.[26] A father in Canada risked arrest when he refused to call his 14-year-old daughter (who received hormone injections against his will) a boy.[27]

People are forced to ask themselves, "Why would they go through that abuse when they could just let it go? Why suffer such loss and abuse?"

Stories filter out to the wider world about Muslims killing Christians after giving them a chance to pray the Muslim prayer and save their lives.

Persecution and martyrdom are vivid testimonies to those of a jaded and self-seeking generation, that there is something worth suffering loss and even dying for. In some circumstances, it is the only way that jaundiced people would ever believe in the Gospel of God and Christ.

I was forcefully struck by this situation in 2017 while walking through the historic university part of the town of Oxford in the United Kingdom. As I passed through the ancient, cobblestoned streets, I thought of the contrast of what was once being taught in this university compared to what is currently being taught in its famed halls.

The university was a Christian innovation, and the central and chief subject was theology. Every other subject revolved around the "queen of sciences" and the entire curriculum reflected a distinctly Christian worldview.

Yet now that same university is a virtual citadel of vain philosophies such as relativism, existentialism, and the humanities; it is primarily coming from an atheistic and humanistic outlook. To the same extent in which universities once offered to enrich and build up the world, they now tear down and destroy through these toxic and empty philosophies.

But standing in the campus plaza is a massive monument to three Christians (Nicholas Ridley, Hugh Latimer, and Thomas Cranmer) who, rather than acknowledge the pope as the head of the church and the mass as an offering of Christ, allowed themselves to be arrested and burnt at the stake. The following account describes the circumstances leading up to the deaths of Nicholas Ridley and Hugh Latimer, taken from *Foxe's Book of Martyrs*.

THE DEATHS OF RIDLEY AND LATIMER
BY JOHN FOXE

THESE REVERED CLERGYMEN SUFFERED October 17, 1555, at Oxford. Pillars of the church and accomplished ornaments of human nature, they were the admiration of the realm, amiably conspicuous in their lives and glorious in their deaths.

Dr. Ridley, born in Northumberland, was first taught grammar at Newcastle and afterward removed to Cambridge, where his aptitude in education raised him gradually until he came to be the head of Pembroke College where he received the title of Doctor of Divinity.

To his sermons the people resorted, swarming about him like bees, coveting the sweet flowers and wholesome juice of the fruitful doctrine which he did not only preach, but showed the same by his life, as a glittering lantern to the eyes and senses of the blind, in such pure order that his very enemies could not reprove him in any one jot. He was a pattern of godliness and virtue, and such he endeavored to make men wherever he came....

When Edward VI was removed from the throne and the bloody Mary succeeded, Ridley was immediately marked as an object of slaughter. He was first sent to the Tower, and afterward at Oxford, was consigned to the common prison of Bocardo, with archbishop Cranmer and Hugh Latimer. . . .

Hugh Latimer was educated at the University of Cambridge, where he entered into the study of the school divinity and was from principle a zealous observer of the Romish superstitions of the time. In his oration when he commenced bachelor of divinity, he inveighed against the reformer Melancthon.

Once converted he became eager for the conversion of others, and commenced to be a public preacher and private instructor in the university. His sermons were so pointed against the absurdity of praying in the Latin tongue and withholding the oracles of salvation from the people who were to be saved by belief in them. Inevitably, he was prohibited from preaching in the churches of the university, notwithstanding which, he continued during three years to advocate openly the cause of Christ, and even his enemies confessed the power of those talents he possessed. Mr. Bilney remained here some time with Mr. Latimer, and thus the place where they frequently walked together obtained the name of Heretics' Hill.

For his sermons here against purgatory, the immaculacy of Mary, and the worship of images, he was cited to appear before the archbishop of Canterbury and the bishop of London.

Thus Master Latimer coming up to London through Smithfield was brought before the Council, where he patiently bore all the mocks and taunts given him by the scornful papists. He was cast into the Tower, where he, being assisted with the heavenly grace of Christ, sustained imprisonment a long time, notwithstanding the cruel and unmerciful handling of the lordly papists, who thought then their kingdom would never fall; he showed himself not only patient, but also cheerful in and above all that which they could work against him. Yea, such a valiant spirit the Lord gave him, that he was able not only to despise the terribleness of prisons and torments, but also to laugh to scorn the doings of his enemies.

Mr. Latimer, after remaining a long time in the Tower, was transported to Oxford, with Cranmer and Ridley. He remained imprisoned until October and the principal objects of all his prayers were threefold: that he might stand faithful to the doctrine he had professed, that God would restore his gospel to England once again, and preserve the Lady Elizabeth to be queen; all of which happened. When he stood at the stake without the Bocardo gate, Oxford, with Dr. Ridley, and fire was putting to the pile of [sticks], he raised his eyes benignantly towards Heaven and said, "God is faithful, who will not suffer you to be tempted above that you are able." His body was forcibly penetrated by the fire, and the blood flowed abundantly from the heart; as if to verify his constant desire that his heart's blood might be shed in defense of the gospel.

Dr. Ridley, the night before execution, was very facetious, had himself shaved, and called his supper a marriage feast. . . . The place of death was on the north side of the town, opposite Baliol College. Dr. Ridley was dressed in a black gown furred, and Mr. Latimer had a long shroud on, hanging down to his feet. When they came to the stake, Mr. Ridley embraced Latimer fervently and bid him: "Be of good heart, brother, for God will either assuage the fury of the flame or else strengthen us to abide it." He then knelt by the stake, and after earnestly praying together, they had a short private conversation. Dr. Smith then preached a short sermon against the martyrs, who would have answered him, but were prevented by Dr. Marshal, the vice-chancellor. Dr. Ridley then took off his gown and tippet and gave them to his brother-in-law, Mr. Shipside. He gave away also many trifles to his weeping friends, and the populace was anxious to get even a fragment of his garments. Mr. Latimer gave nothing, and from the poverty of his garb, was soon stripped to his shroud, and stood venerable and erect, fearless of death.

Dr. Ridley being unclothed to his shirt, the smith placed an iron chain about their waists, and Dr. Ridley bid him fasten it securely; his brother having tied a bag of gunpowder about his neck, gave some also to Mr. Latimer.

A lighted [stick] was now laid at Dr. Ridley's feet, which caused Mr. Latimer to say: "Be of good cheer, Ridley; and play the man. We shall this day, by God's grace, light up such a candle in England, as I trust, will never be put out."

When Dr. Ridley saw the fire flaming up towards him, he cried with a wonderful loud voice, "Lord, Lord, receive my spirit." Master Latimer, crying as vehemently on the other side, "O Father of heaven, receive my soul!" received the flame as if embracing it. After that he had stroked his face with his hands, and as it were, bathed them a little in the fire, he soon died (as it appeared) with very little pain or none.[28]

How We Win by Losing

The deaths of Ridley and Latimer

When I think of the deaths of these three believers, I think what a slap in the face this is to relativism and all of the other modern denials of truth. The monument at Oxford honoring these men, inscribed in 1841, reads:

> To the Glory of God, and in grateful commemoration of His servants, Thomas Cranmer, Nicholas Ridley, Hugh Latimer, Prelates of the Church of England, who near this spot yielded their bodies to be burned, bearing witness to the sacred truths which they had affirmed and maintained against the errors of the Church of Rome, and rejoicing that to them it was given not only to believe in Christ,

> but also to suffer for His sake; this monument was erected by public subscription in the year of our Lord God, MDCCCXLI.

Through this kind of testimony, godless people are forced to see there is truth worth dying for instead of denying that same truth. Trusting in the truth of God is often how we are called to win the spiritual battle in which we, as believers in Christ, find ourselves. To the unbeliever, it may appear that we have lost as we give up our lives for truth, but it is in this "losing" that we have won and gained eternal life.

> And they overcame him by the blood of the Lamb, and by the word of their testimony; and they loved not their lives unto the death. (Revelation 12:11)

Putting on the Armor of God

Wherefore take unto you the whole armour of God, that ye may be able to withstand in the evil day, and having done all, to stand. Stand therefore, having your loins girt about with truth, and having on the breastplate of righteousness; And your feet shod with the preparation of the gospel of peace; Above all, taking the shield of faith, wherewith ye shall be able to quench all the fiery darts of the wicked. And take the helmet of salvation, and the sword of the Spirit, which is the word of God: Praying always with all prayer and supplication in the Spirit, and watching thereunto with all perseverance and supplication for all saints. (Ephesians 6: 13-18)

Endnotes

1. See "Bible Commentaries" on 2 Thessalonians 2:11: https://biblehub.com/commentaries/2_thessalonians/2-11.htm.

2. *A Course in Miracles* Preface (Glen Ellen, CA: Foundation for Inner Peace, 1975), https://acourseinmiraclesnow.com/course-miracles-preface.

3 For a listing of Bill Randles books: https://www.amazon.com/Bill-Randles/e/B00IZ5CR2G/ref=sr_ntt_srch_lnk_4?qid=1516487224&sr=8-4-fkmr0.

4. For more information, read *False Revival Coming: Holy Laughter or Strong Delusion?* by Warren B. Smith (online at https://www.lighthousetrailsresearch.com/blog/?p=16760 or purchase through www.lighthousetrails.com).

5. Read *Signs and Wonders! Five Things You Should Consider* by David Dombrowski (online at: https://www.lighthousetrailsresearch.com/blog/?p=21222 or purchase through www.lighthousetrails.com).

6. Written about in Kenneth Copeland's book, *The Force of Faith;* https://my.kcm.org/p-245-the-force-of-faith.aspx.

7. In Kenneth Copeland's magazine, *Believer's Voice of Victory*, Vol. 19, No. 9, Sept. 1991, this belief was promoted: "For three days He suffered everything there is to suffer. Some people don't want to believe that. They want to believe that after His death, Jesus just stayed in that upper region of Sheol that the Bible calls paradise, but they're mistaken! If He had simply stayed there, there would have been no price paid for sin."

8. From *Believer's Voice of Victory*, Vol. 19, No. 9, Sept. 1991, "The Price of It All," p. 3, Kenneth Copeland: "He [Jesus] allowed the devil to drag Him into the depths of hell . . . He allowed Himself to come under Satan's control . . . every

demon in hell came down on Him to annihilate Him . . . They tortured Him beyond anything anybody had ever conceived. For three days He suffered everything there is to suffer."

9. "You are as much the incarnation of God as Jesus Christ was . . . the believer is as much an incarnation as was Jesus of Nazareth"; Kenneth Hagin, *Word Of Faith*, December, 1980, p. 14.

10. Bill Randles, *Mending the Nets: Themes and Commentary of First John* (St. Matthew Publishing, 1999), pp. 39-40.

11. Mike Oppenheimer, "What is Gnosticism?" (Let Us Reason Ministries, http://www.letusreason.org/Current48.htm).

12. Kenneth Copeland, "What Satan Saw on the Day of Pentecost," audiotape #BCC-19, side 1.

13. Kenneth Copeland, "Substitution and Identification," 1989, tape #00-0202, side 2.

14. F.V. Scott, "John Wimber and the Vineyard Ministries" (*Passport* magazine), p. 19.

15. John Wimber, "Ministering in England" Audio Tape (Media Spotlight Report); John Goodwin, "Testing the Fruit of the Vineyard" (Media Spotlight Report, 1990).

16. Bill Randles, *Weighed and Found Wanting: Putting the Toronto Blessing in Context* (St. Matthews Publishing, 1995), p. 81.

17. Anugrah Kumar, "Bethel Church Responds to 'Christian Tarot Cards' Controversy" (*Christian Post*, January 6, 2018; https://www.christianpost.com/news/bethel-church-responds-christian-tarot-cards-controversy-212796.

18. Ibid.

19. Ibid.

20. Alfred Edersheim, *The Life and Times of Jesus The Messiah*, book III, chapter 1 (Grand Rapids, MI: Eerdman's Publishing), p. 686.

21. Maddy Savage, "Thousands Of Swedes Are Inserting Microchips Under Their Skin" (NPR, October 22, 2018,

Endnotes

https://www.npr.org/2018/10/22/658808705/thousands-of-swedes-are-inserting-microchips-under-their-skin).

22. Philip Pullella, "Middle East Needs Two-state Solution, Pope Says in Christmas Address" (*Reuters,* December 25, 2017, https://news.yahoo.com/mideast-needs-two-state-solution-pope-says-christmas-113127490.html).

23. "Pope Francis' Address To The United Nations" (https://newyork.cbslocal.com/2015/09/25/pope-francis-united-nations-speech-full-text).

24. Bill Randles, "How They Gain the World," Part 4 (https://billrandles.wordpress.com/2018/02/26/how-they-gain-the-world-mark-8-pt-4).

25. Caitlin Burke, "Oregon Bakers Lost Everything Before Even Going to Court, Now Their Voice Is Heard" (CBN, March 2, 2017, https://www1.cbn.com/cbnnews/us/2017/march/oregon-bakers-lose-everything-before-ever-going-to-court-today-that-changes).

26. Leah MarieAnn Klett, "Kim Davis Tells Her Side of the Story, Says Mainstream Media Painted 'Unfair' Picture" (*Christian Post*, March 16, 2018, https://www.christianpost.com/news/kim-davis-tells-her-side-of-the-story-says-mainstream-media-painted-unfair-picture-exclusive.html).

27. Jeremiah Keenan, "Authorities to Arrest Canadian Father if He Refers to Trans Child as Her Real Sex" (*The Federalist*, April 29, 2019, https://thefederalist.com/2019/04/29/authorities-arrest-canadian-father-refers-trans-child-real-sex/).

28. John Foxe, *Foxe's Book of Martyrs* (Eureka, MT: Lighthouse Trails, 2010, 5th printing 2017), pp. 239-243.

Scripture Verse Index

Numbers

1 John 2:14 66
1 John 2:15-18 55
1 John 2:21 45
1 John 3:7-8 44
1 John 4:1-3 31
1 John 4:1-4 16
1 John 4:1-6 38
1 John 4:4-5 36
1 John 4:6 38
1 John 5:5-6 42
1 John 5:19 90
1 John 5:19-21 53
1 Peter 2:24 40
1 Peter 3:18 40
1 Timothy 4:1-3 23
2 Corinthians 11:2 83
2 John 1:1 83
2 Peter 3:10-13 58
2 Thessalonians 2:8-12 17
2 Thessalonians 2:10-12 35

A

Acts 1:8 90

D

Daniel 7:20-22 8
Daniel 9:25-27 32
Daniel 10:26 103
Daniel 11:32-35 104

Deuteronomy 6:16 67
Deuteronomy 8:2-3 61

E

Ephesians 6:11 64
Ephesians 6:12 69
Exodus 17:7 67

G

Galatians 1:4 55
Genesis 3:1 11
Genesis 3:2 12
Genesis 3:3-4 13

H

Hebrews 9:27 20
Hosea 5:15 87

I

Isaiah 1:21 83
Isaiah 14:12 18
Isaiah 24:5, 21 76
Isaiah 43:10 22

J

James 4:4 55
Jeremiah 31:35-37 87
John 5:43 33
John 10:10 85
John 15:18-19 55
John 18:37 38

L

Luke 4:6 68
Luke 12:1 91
Luke 12:2-3 92
Luke 12:4-5 93
Luke 12:6-7 93
Luke 12:8-9 94
Luke 12:8-12 97
Luke 12:10 91
Luke 12:11-12 89
Luke 22:53 57

M

Mark 9:43, 48-49 15
Matthew 4:3 60
Matthew 4:5-7 64
Matthew 4:7-10 68
Matthew 8:12 15
Matthew 13:41-42, 49-50 15
Matthew 22:13 15
Matthew 22:37 70
Matthew 24:10 101

P

Psalm 2:1-4 73
Psalm 48:1-6 77
Psalm 91:10-12 66

R

Revelation 6:15-17 79
Revelation 11:15 69
Revelation 12:1-4 81
Revelation 12:3 9
Revelation 12:4 85
Revelation 12:5 84
Revelation 12:9 12, 18, 84
Revelation 12:11 108
Revelation 12:12 10, 86
Revelation 12:15-17 88
Revelation 13:4-8 7
Revelation 14:7-11 72
Revelation 16:13-14 78
Revelation 19:7 83
Revelation 19:19 79
Revelation 19:20 71
Revelation 21:9 83
Romans 1:21 70
Romans 6:23 40

Z

Zechariah 9:9 83

Other Resources by Bill Randles

Beware the New Prophets | 232 pages | $15.50 | Believers in Grace **Publishing**

God Remembers: The Visions and Words of the Prophet Zechariah | 160 pages | $14.95 | **Believers in Grace**

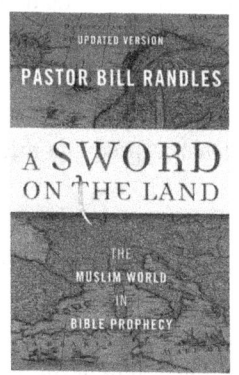

A Sword in the Land: The Muslim World in Bible Prophecy | 260 pages | $15.50 | **Believers in Grace**

Beware of Bethel: A Brief Summary of Bill Johnson's Unbiblical Teachings | 14 pages | $1.95 | Lighthouse Trails

The resources on this page can be purchased through Lighthouse Trails.

Other Books by Bill Randles

Making War in the Heavenlies: A different look at Spiritual Warfare (1994) Bill Randles was asked in 1994 to explain why he wasn't leading his church into various aspects of city-wide spiritual warfare exercising, such as prayer walking, March for Jesus, naming the demons over the city, binding and loosing, etc. Out of that explanation came this book, which discusses not only the heretical practices listed above, but the true biblical teaching on spiritual warfare.

Weighed and Found Wanting: Putting the Toronto Blessing in Context (1995) Thousands of Christians were traveling to the Toronto Airport Vineyard to experience "a new anointing," and Spiritual Drunkeness. Was this really "as a rushing mighty wind from heaven" as its proponents claimed? Bill refutes this notion, having traced the "revival" back to its roots in the Manifested Sons of God heresy, once rebuked and rejected by the Assemblies of God, but now widely accepted as a mighty revival.

Born From Above: An Exposition of John Chapter 3 (2015) This is an exposition of the third chapter of the Gospel of John, one of the most familiar and beloved chapters in the New Testament. In this brief study, Bill shows the continuity of the theme, the New Birth as taught by Jesus, in a conversation with one of the greatest and most renown theologians of his day, Nicodemus. Pastor Bill sheds new light on familiar texts such as John 3:16. This book is expositional and evangelistic as well. It would be great for Bible studies.

Mending The Nets: Themes and Commentary of First John (1999) In this book, Bill explores the undergirding themes of first John, such as eternal life, the tests of eternal life, true and false faith, the Gnostic redefinition of the knowledge of God, and the true knowledge of God. Like John, Pastor Bill takes us back to the beginning, the first thing revealed in the Gospel of Jesus. This commentary is relevant to the current apostasy in the church.

A Sword On The Land: The Muslim World in Bible Prophecy (2013) The 2011 "Arab Spring" was significant, but not for the reasons the world hoped for. Bill Randles, in a very readable style, explains that rather than being a movement towards democracy in the Arab world, the real significance was the setting in place of the nations of the Middle East for the fulfillment of end-times prophecies. (Available through Lighthouse Trails, see page 121 for details.)

Creation, Fall, and the Hope of Redemption (2016) A verse-by-verse commentary of the foundational book of the Bible, Genesis 111. Bill takes the reader through a devotional and informative tour of the Creation, fall of man, Cain and Abel, the creation of the first city, the development of civilization, the conditions leading to the flood, and the Tower of Babel, and the division of humanity. This book shows us that not only are the early chapters of Genesis about our beginnings but they also foreshadow the end times and final judgments of the Lord upon this Earth. But the book is also a testament to the salvation of God, right from the beginning, through the seed of the woman promise, which is the key to unlocking all of the Book of Genesis.

The books on these two pages can be ordered through Amazon or www.believersingrace.com (319-373-3899).

TOPICAL BOOKLETS FROM LIGHTHOUSE TRAILS

Lighthouse Trails Booklets are topical booklets designed to share with others important truths from a biblical perspective.

What is so wonderful about these Booklets is two-fold: one, we are selling them at very low prices so just about anyone can afford to buy them (with quantity orders of the same title, the discount is as much as 45% off retail); and two, we are told when they are being handed out to people by our readers, people are reading them. That's the best news of all!

Each Booklet is between 10-18 pages and is written by one of the 35 authors Lighthouse Trails Publishing represents. The booklets can be purchased individually or in bulk at very affordable prices and given out.

Each Booklet is $1.95 retail with the following discounts:

6-25: $1.66; 26-50: $1.46; 51-100: $1.28;

and 101 or more: $1.07

140 BOOKLETS TO SHARE WITH THOSE YOU CARE ABOUT
FULL COLOR, COMPELLING COVERS
BOOK-SIZE DIMENSIONS (8.5" X 5.5")
10-18 PAGES LONG
VITAL INFORMATION INSIDE!
(And Plenty of Documentation)

OTHER BOOKS BY LIGHTHOUSE TRAILS

A Time of Departing
by Ray Yungen, $14.95

Calvinism: None Dare Call It Heresy by Bob Kirkland, $11.95

Changed by Beholding
by Harry Ironside, $11.95

Father ten Boom, God's Man
by Corrie ten Boom, $13.95

For Many Shall Come in My Name by Ray Yungen, $13.95

Foxe's Book of Martyrs
by John Foxe, $14.95, illustrated

How to Prepare for Hard Times and Persecution by Maria Kneas, $14.95

How to Protect Your Child From the New Age & Spiritual Deception by Berit Kjos, $14.95

In My Father's House
by Corrie ten Boom, $13.95

Muddy Waters
by Nanci des Gerlaise, $13.95

Out of India
by Caryl Matrisciana, $14.95

Seducers Among Our Children
by Patrick Crough, $14.95

Simple Answers: Understanding the Catholic Faith by Ray Yungen, $12.95

Stories from Indian Wigwams and Northern Campfires by Egerton Ryerson Young, $15.95

Strength for Tough Times, 2nd ed. by Maria Kneas, $11.95

Taizé—A Community and Worship: Ecumenical Reconciliation or an Interfaith Delusion? by Chris Lawson, $10.95

The Color of Pain
by Gregory Reid, $10.95

The Trinity: The Triune Nature of God by Mike Oppenheimer, $11.95

Things We Couldn't Say
by Diet Eman, $14.95, photos

The Gospel in Bonds
by Georgi Vins, $13.95

The Other Side of the River
by Kevin Reeves, $12.95

Trapped in Hitler's Hell
by Anita Dittman, $14.95

For a complete listing of all our books, DVDs, and CDs, go to www.lighthousetrails.com, or request a copy of our catalog.

NOTES

To order additional copies of:
War Against the Saints
Send $11.50 per book plus shipping to:
Lighthouse Trails Publishing
P.O. Box 307
Roseburg, Oregon 97470
(U.S.Shipping is $3.95 for 1 book;
$5.25/2-3 books; $10.95/4-20 books)

You may also purchase Lighthouse Trails books from www.lighthousetrails.com. For a complete listing of all Lighthouse Trails resources, request a free catalog.
For bulk rates of 10 or more copies (40% off retail), contact Lighthouse Trails Publishing, either by phone, e-mail, or fax. You may also order retail or bulk online at www.lighthousetrails.com, or call our toll-free number:

866-876-3910 (USA/CA)
For international and all other calls:
541-391-7699
Fax:541-391-7697

War Against the Saints, as well as other books by Lighthouse Trails Publishing, can be ordered directly through Lighthouse Trails.

Visit our research site at www.lighthousetrailsresearch.com.
You may visit the author's website at:
https://billrandles.wordpress.com.

www.ingramcontent.com/pod-product-compliance
Lightning Source LLC
Chambersburg PA
CBHW061446040426
42450CB00007B/1243